Deceived *from* Within

Deceived
from Within

Living with APS and Lupus

DARREN RADKE

iUniverse®

DECEIVED FROM WITHIN
LIVING WITH APS AND LUPUS

iUniverse books may be ordered through booksellers or by contacting:

iUniverse
1663 Liberty Drive
Bloomington, IN 47403
www.iuniverse.com
844-349-9409

ISBN: 978-1-6632-2293-0 (sc)
ISBN: 978-1-6632-2294-7 (e)

Library of Congress Control Number: 2021909712

Print information available on the last page.

iUniverse rev. date: 06/10/2021

CONTENTS

INTRODUCTION

"The best way to predict the future is by creating it."
(Author Unknown)

My life was progressing, moving forward, both personal and professionally. Then April 2000 hit, and with it, two blood clots. What happened? How did I develop blood clots when I am perfectly healthy? Years would pass with no concrete answers or an official diagnosis. Due to blood thinners, I had restrictions, what to avoid, what to watch. Yet, I could continue the day-to-day normalcy in my life. My routine stayed the same. I still controlled every aspect of my life.

Then I woke up one morning and out of nowhere, my entire body changed. Changes that were above and beyond my blood clot issue. And with the changes, anxiety and depression set in. Forgetfulness, brain fog, an inability to understand conversations. Daily bouts of fatigue. The painful headaches. The sensitivity to the sun. My health has dismantled pieces of my wellbeing. I no longer had control of my life.

What could I do? I was suffering unexplained health issues that were taking apart pieces of my life that I fought so hard for. My body was stuck in neutral, and I could not shift gears. Pleaded with my doctors for help. None came.

It took years before help arrived. Through an unlikely source. One phone call. Advice to research a website: www.apsfa.org. To thoroughly read. And sure enough, that advice changed my entire life. A phone call to the administrator was all it took. Answers I was looking for. In 2012, doctors diagnosed me with two autoimmune diseases, APS (Antiphospholipid Syndrome) and Lupus (Systemic Lupus Erythematosus). The doctors found a 3mm x 3mm cyst against my hippocampus, lodged in my brain. All three affecting my Central Nervous System. The ultimate trifecta.

APS and Lupus may have knocked me down, but not out. The precursor from losing jobs because of my life changed with a positive disability verdict. Slowly, I would regain signs of normalcy in my life. There are still struggles. They will never disappear. At least I know what I am up against. I got to keep fighting. And I continue to live within my boundaries. My health boundaries.

After years on disability, I started drafting a short story for the APS website. Only problem, writing about myself is not one of my strong suits. You are sharing things you would not want to tell your family. Or your neighbors. Friends. Yet something changed. And I do not know exactly why.

Over the years, I have added more to my story. Adding bits and pieces along the way. That is when the book idea kicked in. I wanted to take my time to think things through. I want words that reflect my strength and character. To pinpoint my true feelings. Key details in my life. The trials and tribulations I have faced. The continuation of my health issues. I live an interesting life. A colleague of my wife read my manuscript and pressed me to keep going. Her words were, "your story needs to be told." And it does.

I like challenges, but drafting a book was more than I wished for. Wow. Writing is hard. How do people do this every day? And how do they ensure they use the right words to reflect the actual experience? I struggled. I rewrote then rewrote again. It is like tennis, the ball continuously going back and forth. And believe it or not, there were even more revisions after that. Writing is hard enough without my chronic health issues. The brain fog and memory loss.

However, I persisted.

This book is significant for me. I need you, the reader to understand the bizarre tale of my illnesses and the enormous changes in my day-to-day life it produced. I went from working for the global company Nike to living on disability. Life's successes and the failures. Losing jobs. The lack of answers after dozens of doctor appointments. The constant unknown of what is going on within my body. I cringe when I think about the money we spent on medical bills.

It is heartbreaking when I think about the memory lapses. Balancing a checkbook on a monthly budget becomes trivial. I cannot do it. And not from a lack of trying. Too many discrepancies. Once, I have helped my wife by writing down numbers, and I made mistakes. She could say "$12.50", yet my brain would process it as "$15.20. Why?

Or botching my daughter's birthday. I often use the 26th as her official day when it is the 23rd. A father should not be screwing up his daughter's birthday. Or I could be driving through a city with my wife, both of us looking for a great place to eat. Select a new place. Be adventurous. Ask her about trying the new restaurant. She will turn to me and say, "We already did." Huh. When was that? Was it good? Was it expensive?

My memory issues attributed to losing my job at my last employer. Consistently printing the wrong names, transactions, numbers, entering information in the computer, etc. My mistakes cost the company revenue. And my performance did not meet the company's standards. I left them no choice but to move forward without me.

Even my memory issues affected my writing. Our desk was littered with sticky notes and half written notebook papers. Being disorganized happens to be one of my biggest pet peeves. You let it sit and you will forget. Thank God for Voice Memos on my phone.

It is difficult as no one can see your issues. The shame, the loneliness, the paranoia. Questioning myself, like, do people believe me? Do they feel sorry for you? Do they see you as someone who wants attention? Do they see you as a bum that does not want to work and freeload off the government? Do they find anger, even humor in it? Would it be better if I were handicapped so doubters can see? Attention all doubters: You are only one bad day away from being me.

I have heard it plenty of times that there is always someone out there who has it worse than I do, whether health or financial well-being. I understand their pain. But I have my moments when I get very emotional. Sad and depressed, feeling sorry for myself. Sometimes I am downright mad. I feel cheated in life. Why do others get to enjoy a normal life when they treat people like crap? Cheated? Flaunt their good fortunes? It is not right.

You are reading about a lonely guy who feels isolated to the World. I do not get out much. Limiting my driving to a minimum due to my health. An introvert. Rarely do I reach out and talk to someone. My body dictates what I can do every day of my life. Cannot help but feel locked up. Crazy to think that it has been ten years and counting. It is rough to accept. Mentally, those conditions take a toll. Yet, I stayed the course. Reasons why I consider myself a strong person. I learned how to be tough. Let my strengths help guide me. Takes time to learn.

Of course, this project has been cathartic for me, but what I really want is to help others who may spend years, like I did, figuring out what is wrong inside of them. I want to reach them to tell them their illness is not invisible. I want to help them find their voice. I want to connect with them so that they might avoid the loneliness, anger, and even shame I have felt or often still feel.

As I end this Introduction, there is a matter of importance I need to discuss. I have written "I believe" when describing details from my past. Essential information happens to be missing from my memory. I would rather use the line "I believe" instead of explaining something that happened that I nor someone else can prove beyond a doubt. People who are no longer in my life to ask, "Did this really happen?"

As you read my story, I want to confirm the feeling of being "Deceived from Within." And with that, I hope the feeling might fade for all of us.

ONE

APS & Lupus

"It's the epic clash when an irresistible force
meets an immovable object."
Author Unknown

I t is best to start this Chapter by saying; I am NOT an autoimmune disease expert. Nor will I try to be. However, I can start by saying that there is no cure for either autoimmune disease. Medications can help those who have one or both to lead every day, active lives. But those medications can only do so much to help. And might do more harm than good. Some days, no matter what you do, you are downright sick. Feeling like a semi-truck hit your body and dragged a few miles down the road. Ouch.

Your body can change in an instant (ex. -Lupus flare-ups). You may wake up feeling fine, but an hour or two later, you feel terrible. Or right away. My morning ritual includes sitting on the couch with my iPhone in hand and a cup of coffee on an end table. Within thirty minutes, I may fall asleep. No warning. Chronic fatigue rearing its ugly head. Then there are days when I feel awful the entire day. And the next day. And the following day as well. So much for getting anything accomplished.

Someone made a fantastic analogy concerning Lupus. Imagine you went out with friends and partied (drinking?), having yourself a good time. Ignoring time. Not a care in the world! You wake up the next morning tired, suffering from brain fog and a headache. Now, take away going out the night before. No partying, no late night. You did absolutely nothing. That my friends are a perfect Lupus analogy. Wish I thought of this analogy first.

Lupus is a pain in the butt, figuratively. I used to love Summer. All the activities. Going to the beach with my family. Swimming, camping, playing golf. I could go on and on. Right now, I hate Summer. I have had to cancel activities. Get-togethers with family and friends. If I have a blistering headache and body aches, I do not want to be outside. I could vomit as a passenger in a car. I feel like I let people down. One moment you are saying yes to plans and the next moment not. Once again, you are a victim of circumstances. Do people understand the changes you make? I hope so for friendship's sake.

I usually will have both unexplained fever/headache and extreme fatigue together. A pounding headache while tired/fatigue is typical for me. Sometimes my head hurts so badly that I cannot sleep. I pray to God to kill me. They hurt! A ten out of ten on the pain measurement scale. Due to stomach lining issues, I can only take acetaminophen for any pain. When my headaches become intolerable, I take three extra-strength acetaminophens and one baby aspirin. No clue what this combination may do to my body. Within an hour, occasionally two, the pain subsides enough for me to sleep. No two days are alike other than waking up with a slight headache and fatigue. More times than not, the headaches disappear. The exhaustion comes and goes throughout the day. However, I have found that the afternoons are becoming tougher to manage. If I sit down for an hour, I can fall asleep quickly.

There are days when just getting out of bed is difficult. My joints can hurt as they are inflamed due to Lupus. One of the worst areas for pain and discomfort is in my spine, the entire spine. My neck to my butt. No matter what I do, my spine hurts. Whether I stand, walk, sit, or lay down, there is pain. I cannot get comfortable. And there is no way I am taking painkillers! No way. I do not need their side effects. My brain can trigger similar feelings of buzzed, floaty, haziness on its own.

If you look at both of my shins, my right looks different from the left. For some odd reason, I have "freckles," discolored areas that appear all over my right shin. And it can burn and itch. Usually at night while sleeping. I have tried skin moisturizer, anti-itch lotions and creams to no avail. Someone from a Lupus Facebook page said jock-itch spray works the best. What? Out of desperation I tried it. Drastic times call for drastic measures. As funny as it may sound using the spray, it worked. Time to go back to bed and sleep.

For the last few years, I have had trouble writing cursive. My hand will be bouncing around uncontrollably. Until recently, I am starting to experience numbness in my hands when I wake up, continuing throughout the morning. An hour or two. What an unusual sensation. I cannot type anything while on my iPhone or computer. Using the mouse for my computer becomes a challenge. I am all over the place. One morning, I nearly dropped my precious Green Bay Packers coffee cup. Now that would be upsetting.

Since my handwriting can be hit or miss, I started using the Voice Memo app on my phone. An app that sat empty is now one of my best friends. Using this app helps me convey my thoughts instantly, instead of running for paper to write my ideas down. The app does not have a problem with my raspy voice. I wish my computer could do the same. Unless I swear. Then it works.

APS can be very scary. Hence, my blood clots. What started off as a generic diagnosis, years later gained an official name, APS, which stands for Antiphospholipid Syndrome. Also known as Hughes Syndrome. Simply, my blood produces too many antibodies and affects healthy organs. My blood is considered too thick, hence APS' alternative name "Sticky Blood." It is a possibility APS caused my heart valve condition, Aortic Valve Regurgitation. There is no scientific proof or testing results. But it cannot be 100% ruled out.

APS and MS (Multiple Sclerosis) have many similarities. One of the biggest is communication. Participating in conversations can be challenging. Quicky, I get off subject, deviate into my own little discussion. Just rambling on, not knowing what I am talking about. I have been lucky on a few occasions, catching myself and telling others that, "I do not know where I was going with that." I end up apologizing to those around me. I cannot help thinking what a moron I must portray to those involved.

I struggle with my thought order. And immediate issues with your pronunciation. This happens a lot, more than I notice how others speak. Or I simply end up with frozen speech. I have the words on the tip of my tongue, but I cannot generate my voice to work. Some people, jokingly will say, "Come on Darren, spit it out." Trust me, I am trying.

Comprehension has always been an issue for me. When it came to leaning, I was better seeing than reading the instructions. Now, not so much. I find instructions, whether verbal or in writing can be tough. My body's natural thought process turns into brain fog. Where you do not know what is going on around you. Brain fog is unique and can be compared to buzzed while drinking alcohol. Everything is out of sorts and no longer clear.

Brain fog reminds me of this antidote. We all have walked into a room and forget why we went there in the first place. Naturally, you turn around and leave. Walk away and then the light goes on. "Now I remember!" Suddenly, you turn around and walk back into the room. However, by the time you walked in, you forgot again. Episodes of brain fog drives this process. It is a headscratcher.

For over twenty years, I have been experiencing bouts of blurry vision, in some cases containing dizziness or nausea. Some last for mere seconds, some minutes. I have had plenty of partial eye disturbances throughout the years. Here is a great example what is occurring: Place your index finger under the bottom of your eye. Raise your finger up, covering half of your eye. That is what this sensation feels like. Thankfully, I have not suffered one in years. I have talked to multiple neurologists about my episodes affecting my vision, to no avail. No answers. Add this to this list of unknowns why my mind is a mess.

I have become a House Husband. I never knew that this title exactly existed until a few years ago. I took on tasks around the house that my wife and I would share (ex. – Laundry). I find myself doing things like run errands that are in-town, like gassing up our vehicles, going to the post office kind of things. We keep a dry erasable board that lists the week's activities. My "Honey-do" list. Outside of doctor appointments or vehicle maintenance appointments, I am at home. No unnecessary driving as the memory issues could arise. Or confusion. Lightheadedness. Dizziness. Deja-vu. I need to be careful, live within my boundaries. I accept that my body dictates my entire life to a certain degree. There happens to be more that I want to accomplish in life. This book for starters. Watching my children graduate high school, celebrating my 25th wedding anniversary, etc. Too much to list.

What will life have in store in the future? My focus is on today. Accomplish all my body allows me. My body and the unpredictability it may cause. Live for today. Seize the day.

TWO

The Unknown Road

"Two roads diverged in a wood, and I, -I took the one
less traveled by, and that has made all the difference."
Robert Frost

Hard to believe that it has been two decades since my health issues began. A ride of fright, stress, and bitterness. Damaging my dignity, my purpose, and my dreams at the same time. I cannot help but wonder if problems were brewing before my blood clots. In my teens? I recall having an issue with bruises covering my arms during eighth grade football. As a left tackle along our offensive line, blocking was my only assignment. I was not afraid to hit. That is the whole point of football. My motto: Hit or be hit. Football is a physical, violent game. A risk–reward scenario. As a player, I needed to accept the bumps, bruises, and muscle strains/fatigue. Eight weeks' worth of football. I suffered bruises all along my arms. New bruises on top of old bruises. The end of the year awards supper, I won an impromptu award. My forearm pad that read, "85 Bruiser Award". Did this award come at a cost? Considering all the bruises I suffered, was this a warning of things to come?

In late 1994, I worked at an auto body repair center. Within a month, even with the proper equipment needed to work in this environment, I looked pale. I was out of it. Felt like I have been drinking and feeling buzzed. I constantly called in sick. Because of attendance issues, they fired me. Was it in an environment filled with toxic chemicals such as paint causing my issue? Did I have a faulty mask? I will never know. Since then, I consistently get floaty, haziness around fumes. From gas to paint, lacquer, to cigarette smoking.

Life drastically improved months after the auto repair center debacle. A company, twenty miles from where I lived hired me as their Shipping and Receiving Manager in 1995. My first management opportunity. However, the lack of training, my high stress levels endured at a pivotal point. Things were undaunting to learn. Within time, I grew into my own. I made necessary changes to improve our department. Hired new employees. Needed to surround myself with great workers to succeed. We went above and beyond expectations. To become the strength of the company.

The date, January 25th, 1997, is a date that will go down in infamy. It would be the date that I met my future wife, Laurie. We were at a bar, sitting together as a group. Three guys on one side of the table and three girls on the other side. As I sat across from Laurie, there was something about her. A sensation, deep down inside of me, something I have never felt before. It was as if God was telling me, "This is whom I want you to be with." God was right.

The following day, the Green Bay Packers played in Super Bowl XXXI. Years in the making. Finally, an opportunity to bring home the Lombardi Trophy back to where it belongs. Green Bay, Wisconsin, Titletown. The anticipation of the Super Bowl was finally here. And with it, a Packers victory! Beating the New England Patriots 35-21. What a weekend. I was one lucky guy. Meeting Laurie the night before. Then watching my beloved Packers win Super Bowl XXXI. Life could not have proved better.

Six months later, I would move from my hometown and relocate to Oshkosh, Wisconsin. Tough decisions would need to be made. After two and a half years of employment, I placed my two-week notice, my resignation. Leaving behind a great employer, and employees, that I had. But in the end, it was for the best. The owner informed me that I was his best manager he ever had. It made me smile and feel proud. A feeling that still lives with me to this day. It left me the impression that my first managerial experience proved successful. Hopefully, I would carry that success with me.

Oshkosh & Appleton (The Fox Valley) was mostly industrial based, blue-collar working environment. Perfect for open managerial positions. Or so I thought. No managerial positions were open. Made me realize that I over-estimated the areas' job market. Eventually, I found a steady job with an unlikely employer. In April of 1998, I was hired by Nike, Inc., Retail Division as a Shipping & Receiving Supervisor, in Oshkosh, WI at a Retail Store in the Outlet Center. A company that I idolized growing up. The King of the sporting goods world. Watching their commercials on television. The Nike Swoosh. Air Jordan's, the ultimate basketball shoe of its era. Named after basketball great, Michael Jordan. I still remember the commercials for Air Jordan's. Film director Spike Lee played the role of "Mars Blackman" promoted Air Jordan's with Michael. The "Bo Knows" commercials featured two-sport athlete Bo Jackson would soon be premiered on television. The ultimate two-sport athlete who played both Professional Baseball and Professional Football. After the baseball season ended, he would at once start playing football. He was not your average player. He excelled in both sports. The birth of the "Just Do It" era had begun.

My first official day, I was on a plane to Portland, Oregon, to the suburb Beaverton. To my destination, the Nike Headquarters Global Business Academy (GBA). What a beautiful sight to behold. Structured in an open, college like campus. Buildings and offices were everywhere. Buildings named after famous athletes, such as baseball legends Mike Schmidt and Nolan Ryan, tennis star John McEnroe. The Bo Jackson Sports and Fitness Center Building, known as "The Bo," was a sight to behold. Unbelievable! From a distance, you could view a basketball court, surrounded by glass windows on the third floor.

A "Welcome to Nike" event was held on the night of our arrival, inside Steve Prefontaine Hall. A small, yet prestigious building. Highlighted exterior. Inside, memorabilia from Steve's University of

Oregon long distance runner's achievements, medals, and trophies. Pictures and paintings featuring both his university days to the 1972 Summer Olympics. An athlete's dream to be honored with such grace. As the evening ended, you felt accepted. An official Nike employee. Awesome.

Starting the following morning, company training would begin. Five days' worth, covering the Nike Mission. Rules, regulations, the standards before us. Days to follow, we learned the line of products. Footwear, apparel, equipment. The weather was a disappointment. "I believe" the sun made an appearance on two of the seven days. Gloomy and overcast with clouds. In a blink of an eye, Day Seven arrived. Flying home. A quick three-day turnaround and we would be traveling to Tucson, Arizona for in-store training. The type of hands-on training that would help us run our store.

We spent two beautiful weeks in Tucson. We stayed at The Sheraton Inn El Conquistador Hotel & Resort, North of Tucson. A gorgeous place. My hotel room had a magnificent view of the golf course. If only I had my golf clubs.

Our time in Tucson was busy, with long days, full of training. We learned the necessities to be a successful store. Unfortunately, we were too busy to get a chance to fully experience Tucson. All the free time we had would be spent at restaurants and our hotel room.

The two weeks just flew by. It was difficult to leave. You could not have asked for better weather. "I believe" it was sunny with temperatures around 80-85 degrees, with no humidity. Time to get back to reality, Wisconsin weather. Home temperatures in the fifties, the sixties if we were lucky. Just a few weeks shy of Memorial Day weekend. A weekend notorious for awful weather. Rain, cold, and usually wind. Yet, I was glad to be home and no longer living out of a suitcase.

After four days at home, I was back to work. The time had arrived to prepare and set up our new store. Before the products arrived, we were introduced to our Grand Opening (G.O.) Team Members. The Grand Opening Team were people who had extensive backgrounds in their fields. The team leader, Marty, set up plenty of new stores.

And with him, an expert with footwear, one for apparel, and one to set up the back room for storage. Great people to work with and to learn from.

Every morning for two weeks, trucks were backing up to the front doors, loaded with products. The arrival of trucks and products were nonstop. Unloading boxes, pricing the items, learning how to set up the sales floor and the back room. Busy, long days. Come early June, our Grand Opening finally arrived with the doors officially open at ten in the morning.

Working in the back room presented plenty of challenges. Mirroring Tucson's back room did not work for us. Tucson's back room was wide open, with easy access to the rolling shelves. The racks and space were tight as we were in the building's corner. Boxes stacked, awaited pricing and storage, everywhere. Congested, disorganized. And a sliver of room to reach my desk. Rough beginnings. I knew that changes were necessary and devised a plan to restructure the entire back room. Making products quickly accessible. We placed footwear and apparel on opposite sides. Footwear closest to the sales floor. Setting footwear in that area paid off ten-folds. The first of many changes.

The changes implemented were like dominoes, each fell one by one. We developed a new system that would pay off ten folds. Started every afternoon, receiving a fax from our trucking company. The fax listed the purchase orders (P.O.) numbers, products to be delivered the following day. I would go through spreadsheets and break down what products they would deliver. Including the prices. I would write everything down, giving a copy to our footwear manager and apparel manager or their backups. The system would help them rearrange their respective store floor areas. Make room for the new products.

Every morning, the back room transformed into a madhouse. We were machines. We kicked butt and took names. Unloading boxes as fast as we could. Boxes cut open, with the tops exposed, and start pricing. Any high-priced footwear was priority number one. Immediately price the footwear and move them onto the sales floor before the store opened.

After footwear, we would turn their attention to apparel. This system worked perfectly. It was efficient and allowed us to maximize our time management. Simple rule in the retail world. You cannot make money when you have product sitting around, unpriced with nowhere to go. We learned our lesson. And with that, the last domino fell.

Our system caught our district manager's attention, who worked out of our Kenosha Store in Wisconsin. The Kenosha store would always be in the top ten in sales every week. Vast store with plenty of room for our district manager and his office. With his direction, all our stores (I believe eight or nine) within our District would use our system. That was the ultimate compliment.

Once work settled down, I could turn my full attention towards Laurie. I knew she was the one I want to be with for the rest of my life. Once our store opened, I started looking for an engagement ring. And what an adventure! Shopping for a ring was a lot harder than I first thought. Different sizes, shapes, cuts, and obviously, prices. An overwhelming shopping experience.

I already knew the perfect time and place to propose. In a few weeks, we had reservations to stay at a Bed & Breakfast Hotel, found outside of Sturgeon Bay (Door County). Our first night, June 26th of 1998, we had supper reservations at the White Gull Inn, found in Fish Creek. A unique outside experience, including a Scandinavian Fish Boil. Tables placed in an oval around the huge fire pit. The cooks explained every detail of the cooking process. I thought before the boil would start, I would propose to Laurie.

I was nervous. Yet, I found the courage to get on one knee to purpose. And like that, Laurie said yes! We were married on October 16th of 1999. What a magical day! I can still picture Laurie walking down the aisle with her Dad. Her wedding dress was breathtaking. The day flew by so fast that before you know it, you are sitting down to eat. Then the dance. And it is midnight, the party's over. In three days, we were off to Sandals Resorts in The Bahamas for our Honeymoon. Seven fun-filled days with picturesque views. Ideal weather. A beautiful place.

Our store remained steady. During that time, I built a great rapport with our District Manager. When the Kenosha store hired a new shipping and receiving supervisor, the district manager sent her to our store to train with me. She was only at our store for three days. A small window to train. Prior to her arrival, I created a manual that walked you through each process. Reflecting, I considered it an incredible honor to train her.

Our district manager was a great guy. Short, bald, skinny with a mustache. A no nonsense, all business personality. He would spend time at our store every couple of months for three days. He would sit down with every Manager and Supervisor who worked there. When we would find out he would be coming, you would get that look of disappointment from everybody. Kind of like, "oh no, he's coming." I did not have that feeling what-so-ever. When we sat down for our talk, we talked about sports. So much for the "No nonsense, all business personality." He was a giant Chicago Bears and Cubs fan. Me, on the other hand, it was the Green Bay Packers and the Milwaukee Brewers. Deep down, he was a cool guy to know and helped me broaden my career with Nike.

My first opportunity, March of 2000, I would be selected as a the G.O. (Grand Opening) Team Member. Assigned to a four-person team to help set up the new Nike Factory Store in Albertville, MN. An incredible honor to be selected. The experience of it all and the challenge that followed. Nothing that worried me one bit. An advantage was knowing my teammates. The team leader, unbeknownst to me, happened to be a familiar face. Marty, the same person responsible for our store. One plus was that Albertville's new shipping and receiving supervisor was my backup in Oshkosh. Simplifying the training process with his subordinates.

Words cannot express what it was like to be picked as a G.O. Team member. My chance to train all store employees. A "show them what you are made of" moment. I instructed the new staff on the procedures we had in place at our store. How to maximize daily workloads, during peak daily periods. Move products within the back room efficient. Times were busy, putting in long days. Reminiscent of our store during set up.

Halfway through my stay, I woke up Monday morning with my right arm swollen. Weird. I was no stranger to muscle swelling. Though, not in my arm. Sadly, I did not put much thought into it. We had another busy day. And I did not have time to worry about the swelling in my arm. My first warning sign.

The following morning my right arm, still swollen, turned pale in color. Grayish. A headscratcher as I had never experienced paleness in either my arms or legs. Not a pretty sight. Did I hit my arm against something? Was I bitten by a bug or a spider? Again, I ignored my arm as we had another busy day ahead of us. My second warning sign.

With the substantial progress made, we, the G.O. Team members, were given the following day (Wednesday) off. We planned to go to the Mall of America, a place I have never been to. I was looking forward to it. To my dismay, a good time at the Mall of America was not in the plans.

I woke up early Wednesday morning in pain. My left chest was hurting. It felt like my left pectoral exploded. The pain on Wednesday morning was constant. No let up. It did not matter how many Tylenol's I took as the pain was not going away. To make matters worse, I could not lift my left arm above my collar bone. I was miserable, missing the full enjoyment of Mall of America. Not being overshadowed, my right arm was still swollen and pale. I should have done something as we had the day off. Perfect timing to go to a walk-in clinic. But the thought never crossed my mind. My third warning sign.

No change with my sleep. I was lucky to get an hour of continuous sleep. My chest pain would not subside. Finally, I asked if someone could take me to a walk-in clinic. I could not manage the pain and the attention it was taking away from finishing the stores training. One of my G.O. Team members volunteered and took me to a walk-in clinic. I needed to know what was going on.

It was a very odd examination. For beginners, my doctor reminded me of my former high school art teacher. The doctor kept pressing his thumb on my right arm, watching how my arm would react to the pressure. Without any tests, the diagnosis was a strain pectoral. And no idea concerning my right arm. Before leaving, I was instructed to see my regular physician if these two conditions continue. Another rough night would lay ahead for me.

Like Wednesday and Thursday nights, I slept awful. Amazingly, I was still in good spirits as I was going home. Both of my parents greeted me upon arrival at the Appleton airport. After seeing my right arm, both of my parents were concerned. Asking questions and commenting that I should get it checked. But I shrugged them off. After two weeks, I was home and wanted to relax.

Laurie took one look at my arm and we headed to the nearest walk-in clinic. She intuitively knew that something significant had happened and needed immediate aid. I pleaded with her that if my chest and arm do not improve, I would go to the doctor's office on Monday. All I cared to do was unwind from my trip. But to no avail, off to the clinic we go. It was mid-afternoon and thankfully, the clinic was quiet. We did not have to wait long before we were taken into an exam room. During the examination, he asked a fair number of questions while thoroughly examining my right arm. He excused himself from the room, told us he would be right back. The doctor was gone for five minutes and returned. Without hesitation, he instructed us to get to the emergency room. He said they would be waiting for me. Ah, okay.

As soon as we checked in, I was taken back into an examination room. After changing into hospital gear, I was led into an x-ray room. The testing did not take long before I overheard, "There it is." Within minutes, I was placed on a bed and wheeled away. A nurse explained that they found a blood clot in my right clavicle (shoulder). She noted that I would be admitted into the hospital. Wow! Twelve hours before, I left Minnesota and now I am back home in a hospital bed.

Shortly after arriving to my room, I had an IV needle inserted, blood pressure cuff applied, and an oxygen meter on my index finger on me. The nurses were setting my room and equipment at what seemed like a record pace. While nurses were working around me, all I was thinking, "You have a blood clot." It just did not seem believable. I am only 28 years old. Blood clots were for older people. It was not long before my wife arrived in my room. The nurses explained my condition to her. We were both in a state of shock. I felt helpless, both physically and mentally exhausted. Tough to manage in a short time.

Every two hours, a nurse would enter my room to draw blood for a Prothrombin Time Test, which quickly measures your blood clotting time (INR test). One nurse accidentally woke me up while drawing blood. She asked what happened, how did I end up here. As soon as I told her I flew home from the Twin Cities, her head snapped up towards me. While looking me in the eye, she said, "My God, you're lucky the clot didn't rupture while in-flight & killed you."

In an instant, I finally understood the severity of my condition. The news hit me like a ton of bricks. After two sleepless nights, I could honestly say that it terrified me to go back to sleep. All I could think of was, what if I fall asleep but never wake up? My wife, a widow at 27 years old after only six months of marriage. Is this what God had in store for me?

Early the next morning, they performed a CT Scan to examine the issue within my chest. A Pulmonary Embolism (PE) in the upper left lung. The explanation for my chest pain. Now I have with two blood clots. My mind was racing at a hundred miles per hour as I still cannot grasp what is happening to me. Will they find more blood clots? Would they heal? How long would I be there? All I wanted was to be home.

On Monday, my clots dissolved, disappeared, and they discharged me. Upon Tuesday's follow-up visit, the doctor informed me of my overall conditions and a treatment plan. The doctors' diagnosis was "Lupus Anticoagulant," a generic way (my doctor's term) to describe that my blood is too thick, and I need to be on blood thinners for the rest of my life. I needed blood tests (draws) twice a week to evaluate my INR until I sustain manageable levels. The goal was to keep my INR counts at 2.5, a count that continues today.

There were a few health issues, starting shortly after my blood clots. In an instance, episodes of lightheaded/dizziness, followed with small bouts of nausea. It is difficult to describe other than the spinning room aura. The episode may fade away if I cover my right eye. I suffered a few bouts with Vertigo. An awful sensation. A walking sensation while pulled to one side. Mentally, to keep moving forward, I had to lean the other way to continue. What an odd feeling to experience. With a daily regimen of baby aspirin, vertigo ceased. The lightheadedness/dizziness continue today without explanations.

Once life, personal and professional settled down, I was called upon to help the Kenosha, Wisconsin store. Their shipping and receiving supervisor were leaving. It was disappointing news as she was the person I trained at my store. I agreed to come down there for a couple of days. My district manager forewarned me that there were plenty of opportunities to implement changes. My main goal was to make an assessment concerning the flowage of product from the back room to the sales floor. Observing allowed me to see the flaws and where we could make improvements. The back room needed an entire makeover. Changes was necessary to improve overall efficiency.

I found their methods difficult to understand and how disorganized the back room looked. Most of the changes would take weeks before we achieved the desired results. One employee was fired, and another transferred to the sales floor. With their remaining staff, we rearranged their shelved products. Starting with moving footwear closer to the sales floor. Secondly, rearranging mixed apparel into one section. Within weeks, the store's backroom efficiency returned to where things needed to be. After our final meeting, my district manager informed me that he was leaving to work at the Global Headquarters in Beaverton, Oregon. A deserving honor for him.

After the changes implemented in Kenosha, my Nike career would continue to rise. My former district manager called me. I was once again, selected as a G.O. Team member. But this opportunity was special. I would be a G.O. Team member to set up the new employee store at the Nike Headquarters! It was mind blowing to be picked when there is a hundred other shipping and receiving supervisors to choose from. With many closer to Oregon.

Reminiscent to my G.O. Team experience from Albertville, Minnesota, it helps when you know the people you will be working alongside of you. Once again, a familiar face greeted me at the airport. Marty, the team leader. I wonder if he had something to do with my choice. The footwear manager selected worked at Albertville, Minnesota's store. Small world.

It was not long before I spent a week at the Nike Global Headquarters. Back where my Nike career first started. The new employee store had to be four times bigger than my store in Oshkosh. Like all the G.O. Teams I have been a part of, were busy. All work and no play. Much like my first trip to Portland (April of 1998), rarely did I see the sun. The skies were cloudy most of the time. I loved Portland, but the lack of sun would be tough to get used to.

One of the immense opportunities with Nike came about during this week. While sitting down with my old district manager, he offered me a position to work for him. I remember the conversation, but I do not recall the position on his staff. Wow. I am being offered a position to work on the Nike campus. The thought of working at the Global Business Academy was appealing. Of course, there would be added responsibilities. Some outside of my own comfort levels. The biggest hurdle, moving to Portland.

I knew right from the get-go that there was no way Laurie would want to pick up and move. We just started building a life for ourselves in Oshkosh. As much as I wanted to entertain the thought, I told him no. I never discussed it with Laurie to get her input. To this day, I wonder what our lives would have been like if I accepted this position. I still think about it now and then. What would life be like if we moved? Would there have been more opportunities with Nike? Regretfully, I wonder if I made the right choice turning the job offer down. Easy to second guess.

The Summer of 2001 started with jubilation, quickly turned to heartbreak. In July, we found out that Laurie was pregnant. It felt like the timing was right to have children. Oshkosh was going to be the place where we would start a family, raise our children.

A few weeks later, my maternal Grossmutter (German for Grandmother) died. She was the best. 100% German and full of spunk. The oldest of ten children, she was the first in the family to learn English. Sadly, she was the only Grandparent I knew. Love you Grossmutter.

In September, we had an ultrasound appointment to see our future child at the end of the first trimester. We could not wait. I do not think either of us slept much the night before. Off to work and then the ultrasound test to see our baby. We were both on Cloud Nine as we left for work. That Tuesday happened to be 9/11/01. Yes, 9/11 when the whole world as we knew it would change. Our generations' Pearl Harbor.

If mornings were slow in the back room, I would help count the registers' tills to ensure the amounts were correct. We would leave the manager's office door propped open until we finished. Our footwear manager walked in shortly after 8 am while we were counting. He said that a plane hit one of the towers at the World Trade Center in New York. We turned on the television that was in our breakroom, just outside the manager's office. I remember being memorized, watching smoke rising from the tower. Then we watched the second plane crash into the other Tower, live on television.

What on Earth is going on? We were all in shock. Our morning routines unexpectedly were sidetracked for the day. Not that it mattered as the store did not have many customers that day. We were all glued to the television, whether it was at work or home. While the Towers were on fire, the television coverage switches from New York to Washington D.C. as a plane crashed into the Pentagon. Time seemed to stop. You could not make sense of it all. As the television coverage switch back to New York, the first of the two towers came crashing down. Then the second fell. Things would only get worse.

In the shadow of the terrorist attacks, it was tough to separate my shock and anger to the eagerness and excitement upon entering the clinic. I do not remember entering the clinic to being called back for the ultrasound prep. Why remember the in-between stuff when there is more important business at hand? Laurie's Obstetrician-Gynecologist performed what we thought would be a routine ultrasound. However, God had other plans for us.

The ultrasound screen would reveal the gestational (fetal) sac but no fetus. In basic terms, a miscarriage. Laurie ended up with a Blighted Ovum (Anembryonic Pregnancy), a type of miscarriage where the gestational sac continues to grow without a fetus. We were crushed. Both of us were crying. A surgical procedure, Dilation and Curettage (D&C), also known as a Vacuum Aspiration, would be needed to remove the gestational sac in the weeks to come. How cruel to look forward to something only to have your hopes and dreams dashed.

I remember how hard it was calling my mom to tell her the bad news. It was just as tough getting up the next morning and go to work. I could barely hold myself together. After telling my store manager what happened, he sent me home. The same thing happened to Laurie. What good would we be at our jobs that day? Our thoughts were elsewhere, far from focused on our jobs. We ended up spending the day at the Fox Valley Mall in Appleton to get away from everything. A chance to talk somewhere other than home. We both agreed that it would be better to move closer to our families. Time to move on and start anew. No longer working for Nike. If there was any good news, it took less than three months, and both of us had new jobs. Finding a place to live did not take long either. A brand-new duplex in southern Wisconsin. Things quickly fell into place as if it were meant to be. It was time for a brand-new start, in a new area.

THREE
Transitions

"Everything happens for a reason. That reason
causes change. Sometimes it hurts. Sometimes it
is hard. But in the end, it's all for the best."
From quotling.com

Moving is never easy. It is a lot of hard work. The planning. Renting a box van. The packing of boxes and clothes. Questions about the furniture. Having enough people to help. The drive, seventy-five miles due south. Upon arrival, the unloading process. We are officially here. Strangers in a strange land. Transitioning our old lives in Oshkosh to our new lives in Marshall.

Starting anew was stressful. We were months into our new jobs. It took time to be comfortable with our new surroundings. Finding insurance companies to protect your house and vehicles. And the most important, health insurance. I had little time to wait for my health insurance coverage to begin. Which hospitals and clinics do my health insurance cover? The same thing with Doctors and Dentists. What is our deductible, copayments, percentage of coverage? Everything takes time, but time was the essence as I need monthly blood draws for my INR. And I needed a doctor to ensure any medication changes. Consistent INR levels was a must!

When it came time to set up a new Primary Care Physician (PCP), I could not have picked a better doctor. Without a doubt, I had the best primary physicians one could ever have. Doctor Ben. He was in his late forties and did not mess around. He called it the way it is. Respectful, down to Earth and took time to explain things. All of clinics' staff said Dr. Ben would stay late to research his patient's conditions or issues. That was how dedicated he was to his patients and profession. Thankfully, the Clinic he worked at Waterloo, WI, on the other side of town. A three-minute drive from my employer. Quick and easy access.

There was a time when I was sicker than a dog for three days. Ice cold, shivering, coughing, and a mild headache. Miserable. A chest x-ray revealed pneumonia throughout both lungs. Dr. Ben turned to me, said, "You have pneumonia, dude." He sat down next to me, placed his hand on my shoulder, conveyed the message how lucky I was. Waiting longer would have meant an ER visit, a hospital admission. Or worse. Best not to think about it.

By June 2002, we found out Laurie was pregnant. We waited before we told our families. We wanted to be sure. This time no issues. The first-semester ultrasound showed a healthy baby boy. A due date for mid-late January. What an incredible feeling knowing I was going to be a dad. You think of all the cool things to do as a father and son.

Not long before our baby was due to enter this world, our second vehicle, died. No warnings as the car worked perfectly fine the day before. I looked at Laurie and asked what we are going to do. Do we get a used vehicle, not knowing its history? Buy a new car? Either way, we needed to decide.

As we weighed our options, we bought the cheapest brand-new car we could find. A green Kia Rio. The lean, mean green machine. It was as basic as they come. No power windows, cruise control, automatic locks, nothing other than an air conditioner and CD player. Nothing special other than it worked. Buying the KIA Rio was worth every cent. 12-1/2 years with no problems.

Laurie started having labor pains at 10:00 pm on January 19th of 2003. And we are off to the hospital. A few hours later, we were on our way home. It took a little while before things progressed. We returned early morning on the 21st, and this time we would stay. Everything was progressing slowly until the afternoon. They watched Laurie's heart rate continuously for hours. Finally, after their heart rates were getting too low, the Doctor said we were going in, which means an emergency Caesarean Section (C-Section). I was beyond scared at this point. The only thought running through my mind was I going to losing both. The Doctor looked at me and said to do whatever I need to do and get back here ASAP—bathroom break. When I returned, the nurses placed a hospital gown on me, booties, and a mask and led me into the operating room. I sat down on Laurie's left side. She was prepped and ready. At 6:48 pm, our son officially entered this World.

What a moment, unlike anything you have ever experienced. Naturally, I was the first to hold him. I brought him to Laurie, which made for a beautiful moment. All the nurses continuously said, oh, what a beautiful baby. After I cut the umbilical cord, the nurses took him to clean him up, measure him, and make footprints for the birth certificate. Once they propped Laurie up, she got to hold him for the first time. Amazing to think we were now parents.

On the 24th, we were discharged and ready for home. And the weather was ice cold. Nothing unusual for Wisconsin. I opened the front door to let both Laurie and Sean come in. You could not see him as he covered up to protect him from the cold. When we reached the top step, our cat Blue was waiting for us. Once Laurie peeled back everything that was shielding our son from the cold, Blue had to investigate what it was we brought home. He sniffed for about five seconds, got his head back, and casually walked away. Blue was not as excited as we were. He would eventually take a few months to warm up to him. Losing attention can be a hard thing. Most infants barely sleep as they need formula. And he was a terrible sleeper.

In August 2003, I started classes at Madison Area Technical College (MATC) every Thursday night in their Business Management Program. They would hold all classes at their now-closed Downtown Campus. The campus was a couple of blocks from Capital Square.

The very heart of a contained area. You had to park at the ramp directly across from the campus. It would typically take 30–35 minutes, depending upon how busy traffic was. And how full the ramp would be. It should come as no shock that both would fluctuate from week to week.

The Business Management Program was eleven six-week courses varied from essential management to business law to the toughest Project Management. Management classes ended in December 2004 before Christmas break. Sometimes we would have twice a week. Every Tuesday and Thursday for just three weeks. We had to squeeze those classes in before any significant break, like Memorial Day, July 4th, Labor Day, and Christmas. Six classes in a matter of seventeen days! Time management was a must, as I had little time to study.

I would usually get home anywhere between 9–9:30 pm after class. Blue would always be on top of the steps to greet me. Like clockwork, I would stay awake as our son would wake up crying between 10–10:30 pm to eat. As I sat in his room, feeding him his bottle, and rocking him in a rocking chair, Blue would sit up above us. There was a shelf directly to the left of the chair, a foot taller than my head would be. Blue would do this all the time. Remember how I mentioned how their relationship would change? I considered Blue our son's Guardian Angel. He would watch over him like a hawk. Once we finished and placed Sean back into his crib, it was time for bed. I dreaded the thought of getting up around 4–4:30 am as I had to be at work at 6 am. Every day, coffee, or soda. Sometimes both. I direly needed caffeine.

As Sean got older, keeping him entertained and finding the right television show was a laborious task. We were trying to find any cartoons, programs for him to watch. It took time, but he settled on two shows. The first and most important was Thomas the Tank Engine (Train). It was funny to listen to who was narrating most of the shows, comedian George Carlin. That is right. The same man whose stand-up comedy included "The Seven Words You Couldn't Say on Television." Other shows had actor Alec Baldwin narrating. Sean's fascination with trains was an understatement. He would point out railroad crossings, moving or parked trains. It was cute to watch and listen to his excitement. One significant part of being a dad.

The other show he liked was The Wiggles. They have a song called "Fruit Salad" that is next to impossible to get that song out of your head. You would hear "Fruit Salad" at least twice a month. "Fruit salad, yummy, yummy, fruit salad, yummy, yummy." Sean thought it was funny. Neither Laurie nor I thought so. A great torture tactic to drive any parent insane. Please, make it stop.

I was proud as I was a straight-A student in college. And by doing so, I was invited and joined the Phi Theta Kappa International Scholastic Order. On October 4th of 2004, I was inducted into MATC's Chapter of Phi Theta Kappa, Beta Beta Psi. "I believe" you had to have a Grade Point Average (GPA) of 3.75 to get in, and you had to keep a 3.66 GPA throughout your entire college career. It was a great honor to be nominated and recognized for your work and accomplishments.

In the Springtime of 2004, we bought an older pop-up camper. We loved camping. Up until that time, we have using a tent. If it rained, you were worried about leaks. Plus, sleeping on inflatable mattresses were far from comfortable. With a baby, using a tent proved to be impractical. Lack of room to move around, how to place everything. The camper supplied plenty of space and storage that we needed. It was a Godsend to have if we were going to continue camping.

Towards the latter part of 2004, we knew we were starting to outgrow our duplex. If we were going to have another child, then we needed more room. Laurie and I crunched the numbers, created a budget. Draw a line in the sand, not to go beyond what we could afford. Then the search for houses began. Finding the right house at a price we could afford was a daunting and stressful task. We knew a fixer up place would never work as I am not a do it yourself, repair person type of guy. I suck at it. But those are the type of houses that, even though were lower in price, would take years to add the repair or updates we want. With small children, we wanted to avoid those houses at all costs.

About three blocks from our duplex, Brookstone Homes started a housing development, building new homes to buyers' specifications. They offered about a dozen different types of figurations, one or two floors, number of bedrooms and bathrooms from which to choose. Lot size (Land) to pick from. We found one that we liked. But we were not sure if we could afford it. The price was right at the line in the sand, budget-wise. We had dreams of what we wanted to do, but could we do it?

In a few weeks, my company's management team decided to combine both supervisor position and manager position into one. On a Friday afternoon, I had an unscheduled meeting with both our plant manager and the company's president. Oh, no. Friday meetings are never good. A good rule of thumb, if a company is going to let you go, it is best to do it right before the weekend. All I was thinking was, I am getting fired. But just the opposite happened. I was hired for the new position. For me, it would be a promotion and a raise. Wow. I was shocked. The pay raise secured the deal to move forward concerning a new house. We were able to afford exactly what we wanted in a house. July of 2005, our dream house was finished and ready to move in. Again, life just fell into place, like it was meant to be.

A brand-new house had a weird feeling to it. Exactly the way we felt when we moved into our duplex. Before we moved, all that was left was to paint the bedroom walls. We hired a painter to save time as we certainly had our hands full. We asked if he would place a border within our son's bedroom. He said no problem. We scheduled a date and time, as we planned accordingly.

To our dismay, the painter we hired proved to be a horrible decision. Unprofessional. There were bald spots along the walls. Paint along the ceiling, due to a poor job of taping. They did not cover the carpeting as there were paint spots scattered. The border was not smooth out as there were areas that bubbled. One end was hanging down. There was little doubt an inexperienced crew worked for the painter. And tasked to do our house.

When the day arrived to do a walk through with our painter, we expressed our disappointment. While pointing out the poor workmanship, he apologized. Unknown to us, he had two jobs at once. He sent another crew to paint our house. We wrote him a check, probably two-thirds' from what he quoted, and sent him on his way. When all was said and done, we fixed the poor work the painter left behind. In hindsight, we should have saved the money and painted ourselves. Live and learn. On the bright side, by the end of July, we were completely moved in.

The rest of the year, with a couple of exceptions, remained status quo. My straight 'A' streak came to an end—one grade lower on a test. And I continued to ignore my reoccurring lightheaded/dizzy spells without telling my PCP. One most significant bit of news was on the horizon. Laurie was pregnant!

At the beginning of the new year (2006), we found out we were having a girl. It was a scheduled C-Section to avoid what happened the first time. Alyssa was born at 11:04 am on June 23rd. As I held her for the first time, she peed on me. A sign of things to come in life. After cutting the umbilical cord, the nurses brought her over to see her mom. The hospital process remained intact. Two healthy children. Now we had one of each, a boy, and a girl. Precisely what both Laurie and I wanted. Everything was great until October hit. It turned life upside down.

Before going to bed on the night of September 30th, Blue looked lethargic. I noticed he was not eating. I found him in our formal dining room. He was distant and would not approach me. Something that was unusual. I was hoping he would fine by the next morning. I was wrong. Blue looked worse. He was in pain. I could sense something was wrong by looking into his eyes. His way of telling you I am sick and need help. I made an appointment to see our Veterinarian in the early evening. It did not take long before the Vet said that Blue's organs were shutting down. He was dying. There was nothing we could do other than have him euthanized. I watched the entire process. Two shots. One to relax him and the other to help him die. A huge part of me died that night on October 1st. A member of the family has left us.

Life changed for the better in four weeks, precisely on Halloween night. It was the day when we bought a 13-week-old male kitten. His name was Oscar, and his computer chip he had implanted showed that he was born on July 1st. Just a mere eight days away from our daughter's birthday. As a family, mostly Sean agreed to change his name to Thomas. A new member of the family!

In a few weeks, November 2006 was the beginning of how our lives would change forever. While at work, I am sitting in a little room that had a computer with a label printer inside. I would always have the door opened as it was noisy. The company's production manager popped in to talk with me. The production manager noticed I was having trouble talking. I was not making any sense, drooling over myself as I tried to speak. Later I was incoherent to talk to him. The next thing I know, I am strapped down to a stretcher, wheeled outside into an ambulance. From there, I was on my way to an emergency room in Madison. After many tests (I do not know how many), there was nothing wrong. Was it just a fluke? No one knew, including Dr. Ben. Much like in April 2000 when I had my two blood clots, the Doctors had nothing to go on. "I believe" we considered it a onetime occurrence and simply moved on. Could it have been a Mini-Stroke/TIA (Transient Ischemic Attack)? How about a real stroke? I know that is a stretch. Regardless of what it was, it scared me.

I suffered another seizure that "I believe" happened on March 8th. While riding in the car of a sales representative on our way for lunch, I blacked out. To this day, I never found out what happened to my body while I was out. Did I violently shake? Or did I slump over? Or did I have a repeat of the first one in November? Once I came to, I was already loaded in an ambulance at my company's parking lot. I was taken to a different hospital this time. The tests they performed showed absolutely nothing. Two similar health issues, but nothing to show for it. But why?

One month later, I suffered my third "seizure." That is great. All three happened at work. And for the third time, I was driven to a different Hospital. And the third time, tests revealed nothing. "I believe" this when I finally informed Dr. Ben of my dizzy spells. My PCP, Dr. Ben, decided to take things upon himself to get answers.

The first thing he did was to contact a Neurologist. It was not long after the third episode that I was prescribed an antiseizure medication Keppra (Levetiracetam). Dr. Ben made it clear that I need to avoid a handful of things, most importantly, alcohol. Of which I made good until May 20th, the day I graduated from college.

Finally, graduation day is here. It was a lot of hard work, most on Laurie's shoulders. As she did more around the house than I did, the biggest was dealing with the kids. We were waiting for my family to arrive before we left for Madison. My mom & dad, my brother, and his wife and their two kids. Our son came but our daughter did not. She was only 11 months old and certainly needed a nap at the same time.

We arrived at MATC's Downtown location to put on our cap, gowns, and the MATC tassel. If you graduated with Honors, you were given a rope to wear, signifying you as an honor student like me. Since I was a Phi Theta Kappa member, I was given a golden sash with Greek lettering and a golden tassel. Once we were inside The Overture Center and sat down, I tried to find my family. You are not going to see anything with all the stage lights beaming down on you. They would be seated on the second balcony near the video camera person recording. As my name was announced, I could hear my brother and nephew yell out, "Go, Big D!" That was cool to listen to them while walking across the stage. Little did I know that after the "Go, Big D" shout out that "My Daddy" could be heard. You can hear it plain as day on the official MATC Graduation Ceremony DVD. I could watch those 10 seconds repeatedly.

Once all the family pictures were taken, we were off to our house for a celebration supper. I poured Whiskey Manhattan's for my parents. I poured my brother a Jack (Daniels) and Coke, the nectar of the Gods. I decided to make myself one. I hate to see him drink alone. What kind of brother would I be?

I woke up the following morning feeling floaty, that things just seemed out of place. Brain fog. And lots of it. I thought once the coffee kicked in and I am up and around that I will be fine. But I was not. As God as my witness, I felt like this for three days. That

Wednesday, I called my PCP's nurse, Micki, and told her what was going on. She asked a lot of questions, something I expected. She asked if I made any recent changes to my food or drinking habits. I told her that I had a couple of alcoholic drinks on Sunday. After a few more questions, she said she would talk to Dr. Ben and get back to me.

Thankfully by the afternoon, my brain fog was finally wearing off. I could not believe what was going on. Even to this day, I have no idea what went on at work other than a meeting. As I am sitting at my desk, I get told that I have a phone call from the Clinic. I picked up the phone, thinking I would be speaking to Micki. Wrong, it was Dr. Ben, and he was livid. His first words were, "Are you in a big hurry to die? I told you to stop drinking. Mixing alcohol with your medication would have over toxified your body". That is all I remember. Hearing "Are you in a big hurry to die" just stayed with me. He warned me before not to drink, and I did not listen. I would the second time. I was not about to put my life and family at risk. I consider myself lucky there was a second time. I could be dead! Since May 20th of 2007, I have been sober and will stay that way until the day I die.

In early June, I was on the floor playing with Alyssa, who was weeks away from her first birthday! While we were playing, I stood up to help her walk, which was more than less a handheld wobble. I never took notice of where we were until we turned around. As we swung around, my right kneecap took a direct hit to the wall. Ouch. It only took a couple of days until my right calf was reddish and swollen. I better get to Dr. Ben and get this checked out. As I had my appointment that Friday morning, we found a blood clot. Thankfully, it was not in a primary vein that could run throughout my body. I would need to be on crutches for two weeks or until the swelling disappeared. Upon talking to the Vice President about my blood clot situation, it became clear that I was becoming a health risk. This marked the fourth time something significant happened to me in seven months. We agreed to part ways. The company helped me with eight week severance pay and five official letters of recommendation, explaining that I was looking to expand my management skills. I was grateful for everything they did to help me. When I look back at things from a managerial standpoint, I question myself if I could perform the job duties moving forward. I left them no choice but to move on without me.

I never received an official diagnosis concerning the three episodes that I passed out—just guesswork. The first one, I genuinely believe it could have been a stroke. Could I prove it? Either I suffered seizures or transient ischemic attacks, also known as Mini-Strokes. I would lean more towards TIA's instead of seizures. This lack of information or knowledge of what happened still bothers me. I have studied like crazy, looking for any answers to what happened. Deep down, I knew more was happening. Life altering changes were on the horizon. And I was not ready nor prepared for what life was to become.

FOUR

One Crisis at a Time, Please

"There cannot be a crisis next week.
My schedule is already full."
Henry A. Kissinger

What a way to kick off the Summer of 2007. I had no job, with a blood clot in my right calf. On our daughter's first birthday, I put on an act to show both sides of our family that I was fine. If they only knew how broken down, I was inside. I tried my best. If I could catch a break in life.

I found an envelope in our mailbox that was disturbing from the Wisconsin Department of Motor Vehicles (DMV). My driver's license was suspended for six months because of my seizures/loss of consciousness. I needed a signature on my DMV paperwork every six months from my Neurologist to evaluate whether I was stable to drive. How am I going to get to any doctor appointments and job interviews? Thank God for my parents as they drove me to my doctor appointments and job interviews.

My appointment with neurologist #1 was short-lived. I do not know why. He was there to make a first assessment. The doctor ordered two significant tests, a sleep study and an EEG or Electroencephalogram. The sleep study, officially named Polysomnogram (PSG), was easy. Before the test, electrodes would be applied to my head. The electrodes require helium gas to help them stick. But the noxious fumes made me floaty and nauseous. And the electrodes take days to remove. The MSLT, known as a Diagnostic Daytime Multiple Sleep Latency test, "I believe" 3–4 hours. The test results revealed I was not falling into a deep sleep, triggering seizures. They placed me on Clonazepam (Klonopin) to relax at night, an aid to promote deep sleep. The medication worked. However, it is risky to take. If mixed with any type of alcohol, it would kill you.

The Electroencephalogram (EEG) was unpleasant. First, my Neurologist informed me to have sunglasses once I completed the test, as you would be sensitive to light. Second, the doctor recommended having someone drive you home. So, I planned accordingly. Once again, electrodes all over your head. They asked me to remain sitting upright in the chair, as best I could. And to keep my eyes wide open as best as possible throughout the test. The test was simple and did not last long. While in a blacked-out room, lights were consistently flashing at you at different intervals. When the test was over, and the room lights were on, I was ready to vomit. I could not get my sunglasses on, as I had to wait as some electrodes were in the way. With my sunglasses on, I remained sensitive to lights. I was tripping out as streaks of light would fly by. Once again, my parents drove me home. I could not wait to get home to lie down.

On July 10th, I had an appointment with my new neurologist (Neurologist #2). My appointment did not start as well as I hoped. I sat in the waiting room, "I believe" for 30 minutes. A nurse called me back into a small examination room. The nurse took my vitals, information, and promptly left, telling me that the doctor should be in shortly. "I believe" I waited 20 minutes, if not longer. Nothing to do but wait. No magazines or newspapers to read. Why I did not poke my head outside the room to find somebody still is a mystery. Finally, he came in. He took his time reading over my file and went through basic questions. The same questions the nurse asked. I noticed that my neurologist lacked a personality. He never made eye contact, like he was looking past me. All business with his head in the computer screen. He instructed me to make an appointment within six months. And up and out he went. What an odd appointment.

I was more than confident researching open management positions in or near Madison. The Madison area market should supply plenty of opportunities. I was dead wrong. Supervisor and management positions were far and few in between. I sent out at least a dozen resumes for jobs I knew I was perfectly qualified. If I could get an interview, I felt confident that my background and degree would help sell me for the position. Only two interviews between August through September.

The first interview was with two company employees, a member of management, and the plant supervisor. After the interview, the plant supervisor asked which tour to give me. The five-minute or the ten-minute tour. Huh, what does that mean? The interviewer told her a five-minute tour. It was clear that I was not getting the job. I wanted to say to her to "Don't bother as I know what you're going to say," that I did not get the job. I left feeling disappointed. I knew in my heart that I was qualified for the position.

The second interview went perfectly. The interview was one and one. I had the managerial experience the company was looking for. We talked about more than just the manager position. He was teaching me a lesson in hiring practices. As he told me I was perfect for the position, the company he said could hire someone fresh out of college with a bachelor's degree. Train the person and pay them $10,000 less than what I was making at my last job. He instructed me that I was looking in the wrong direction as the Madison area was a white collared area, professional/office positions. Instead, my attention should be towards the Milwaukee area, dominated by blue-collar manufacturing positions. I thanked him for his honesty, and if he reconsidered, I would be more than happy to come back to continue our conversation. No phone call. They were not reconsidering me. My dream of a Management position was quickly fading.

I may have been collecting unemployment benefits, but I needed a job, money, and sanity wise. September passed by without an interview. I called places to no avail. Out of desperation, I was sending resumes to companies for Accounting positions I knew I had no opportunity for the position or an interview.

Thankfully, I had an interview for an open Dispatcher position. My interview seemed to go well. The question asked to be problematic was whether I could reach a CDL (Commercial Driver's License). Unfortunately, I had to break the news about my driver's license. Thought there was no way I was getting the job. Received a phone call from their human resource manager that I may not need a CDL to perform the tasks. Back later in the day and offered the job. Thank God. My first day would be October 15.

My overall duties, responsibilities seemed simple during my training. I had two instructors with both having their own unique scheduling methods. My primary responsibility was to assign the drivers the type of services needed per customer. To assign which container or containers, the customers needed service. Services ranging from new container deliveries, dump the container and return, or simply dump the container and hauled to our facility, as the customer no longer needed our service. Straight forward, attention to detail scheduling. Time-consuming.

I had my second appointment with neurologist #2 on November 12. I was still experiencing the lightheaded/dizziness episodes. But I kept my mouth shut as I had my DMV paperwork and wanted my driver's license reinstated. My appointment was a carbon copy of my first one. He entered and at once turned to the computer monitor. Reading things back to me, asking me if those details sounded right. Am I have been experiencing any seizure-like symptoms? No. I gave him my DMV paperwork and explained that he needed to sign off before driving again. He scanned over the paperwork and at once signed them. It was as if he is no stranger to this paperwork. He instructed me to make an appointment within six months. Sounds good to me. Now I have my license back. Yes!

After the first couple of weeks of work, I started bleeding after bowel movements. My pants would be full of blood around the crotch area. It was not pleasant sitting at work with blood-stained khakis. I figure I better not mess around. Time to call to Dr. Ben and get an appointment with him ASAP.

At the conclusion of my exam, Dr. Ben thought it would be best to have my hemorrhoids banded (rubber band ligation). It is a minimally invasive technique that involves tying the hemorrhoid base with a rubber band to stop blood flow to the hemorrhoids. They scheduled my surgery for November 12. The surgeon made a couple of changes, what foods to avoid and the amount of Warfarin (blood thinner medication) to take every day. Not a great way to start your new job.

I was off from work for a while to rest and recuperate. On the morning of November 26, I started developing stomach pains, the ones that felt like the onset of diarrhea. Instead of loose bowels, I was passing blood. Not a small amount as I am passing a urine type stream. Laurie drove me to the ER to find out what was going on. All it took was an INR test, showing that my blood was dangerously thin. I was taking a dangerous level of Warfarin. A miscommunication between the surgeon and Dr. Ben. Chances were good that if I continued bleeding, I would have bled to death. What a way to go. Me dying due to blood flowing out of my butt like water from a faucet. I would end up spending a couple of days in the hospital until my INR got back to normal. What a scary time.

2008 got off to a lousy start. I was having trouble at work. My performance was anything but stellar. In a few weeks, I felt lost, and it showed. Scheduling errors with customer orders. Mostly concerning the daily scheduling duties for seven to eight drivers. Before you know it, I would work longer hours. After four months, I needed a change. The way things were going, they would fire me. I was already suffering from a lack of motivation, feeling burnt out and overwhelmed with my duties. Like a passenger on the Titanic, I was drowning in the icy waters.

In early April, I received a phone call from my PCP's nurse Micki, out of the blue. What is up with this? Micki gives me the horrible news that Dr. Ben died. My God. Dr. Ben was everything you could want in a doctor. I honestly believe to this day that I would have been able to get answers to my expanding health issues. Dr. Ben would have listened. He could have been an advocate for me. We will never know. Rest in peace, Dr. Ben.

In late April, I met with our human resources manager to discuss an opening for a customer sales representative (CSR) position in the data destruction department (commercial paper shredding). I knew it would be a setback, giving up a managerial position. I enjoyed working there, and I did not want to leave. After a meeting with the company's data destruction department manager, we agreed to the change in positions. It would take a few weeks to make the switch official, but I knew I made the right choice.

I had a routine appointment with my new PCP, Dr. Harris, in May 2008. I do not recall why other than building a rapport with her patients. While speaking with her, I mentioned I had a splitting headache. She asked me a few general questions concerning them, how often they happen, what were you doing when they appeared. I explained to her that most happened during resistant training. Something I usually performed before work. She asked how long my training sessions last. Her next question, how much do I lift, pounds per reps (repetitions). For years, I have always lifted heavy with 6-8 reps. Dr. Harris looked a little concerned and asked how soon the headaches appear while training. I told her at once. Her head snapped up and told me to get to the ER at once. "I believe" she did not say why. She was not messing around. Great. What is happening to me?

Once I arrived at the ER, the medical staff brought me into an examination room. From there, I was led away to have two tests done; Echocardiogram (ECHO) to study my heart's graphic outline movements) and an Ultrasound (high-frequency sound waves), pictures of my heart valves and chambers. Once the testing was completed, I was back to an examination room, waiting for a doctor to discuss my results. I did not take the time to understand why they ran those tests. Never placed two-and-two together.

Little that I know, but a cardiologist would appear into my room. Why a cardiologist? She explained that I had a heart valve that opens and closes irregularly, known as Aortic Valve Regurgitation.

The stress on my heart would create abnormal breathing patterns, making my heart to work harder than it should. When stressed, the heart valve opens and closes irregularly, causing me to have immediate headaches. More than likely, from performing stressful exercising, from running to heavy resistant training. My heart valve could rupture at any moment. Whoa. As a healthy 36-year-old, the news was tough to make sense. I was given a referral and promptly discharged from the hospital.

Starting on May 28, I made the official switch to the data destruction department. The department was small, consisting of the Manager and two to three drivers. My responsibilities were split into two within the company. Meaning answering phone calls, assign them to the right people, setting up new customers, enter all the customer requests into the computer system for our dispatchers for both data destruction and the main function of the company, containers. I had to find a balance between both jobs.

I felt like I belonged in this department and happy I made the switch. There was not a massive fluctuation in my data destruction responsibilities, as they were straightforward. The scheduling of customers and preparing paperwork for our drivers. The paperwork was vital. Once we dumped the containers, the papers would be pulverized into dust. Once the container was 100% empty, the customer would sign our paperwork and receive a copy for their files. The original copy would be placed within our files. Simplistic.

My first cardiologist appointment took place on July 8th. She was friendly, straightforward, and was down to Earth. She took the time, explained my overall heart function. As the appointment ended, she would schedule a CT Scan to see what is happening with my heart valve. As I left, we talked about starting medications to help with my heart, Metoprolol Succinate (Toprol XL) and Amlodipine (Norvasc), respectively. I cringed as I do not want to take more medications. The CT Scan confirmed my heart abnormality, an aortic valve regurgitation.

Time reared its ugly head as I had my neurologist appointment. My third visit with him. But this appointment was nothing like my prior ones. I gathered the courage to explain the reoccurring lightheaded/dizziness episodes. Verbally, he came down on me like a ton of bricks. Immediately, he changed my antiseizure medication. As he wrote a new prescription, he blurts out, "Get ready to pay for the big stuff." Why would any doctor, regardless of their background, say such a thing? Unprofessional.

What I found confusing; he did not order any tests. I wanted to know the reasons I was having periods of lightheadedness and the dizziness. There must be an answer. Do nothing other than prescribe medication. Best to keep my mouth shut and leave the room.

He started me on 800# mg of an antiseizure medicine called Lamictal (Lamotrigine), which was expensive. It was a $50 monthly copay. As I checked medication paperwork, it read my insurance saved me over $300. Excuse me. This medication costs $350 per month. More than double the cost from my current medication.

Not long after, my appointment came time for my year-end review. Time for a raise! Nothing to worry about as I was performing at a high level, meeting the company's standards. Wow was I wrong. Mistakes. And there was plenty. I was making data entry errors, wrong services needed, and quoting/charging customers the incorrect prices. I listened in on some of my phone calls that the company records. There were times I asked the customer to repeat areas I missed, such as their first name. I could not understand why. At the conclusion of my review, my supervisor wanted to go back to the basics, retrain to limit my mistakes. I thanked him and returned to my desk. If there was a plus side to my review, all mistakes occurred outside of my data destruction CSR duties.

As I reflected on the meeting, I realized that was the first time I have ever received a poor job performance review. A blow to my ego and confidence. And to think that all this time my performance was poor. I realized I was failing at something I considered easy. But I knew in my heart the issues would not last. And I was confident that I would turn things around.

2008 was a long year and I could not wait for 2009. Hopefully, the new year would see improvements, avoid any significant issues, whether they were health-wise, work, or family. But I found myself stuck in my behaviors of 2008. I continued having the same issues as before, the memory, comprehension, lightheaded/dizziness episodes. I started having more health issues. The first, partial eye blockages. Even though they would not happen often, it was a concern. Especially when I would be driving. It was as if I was placing my index finger and covering the bottom half of my right eye. Difficult to explain such an unusual phenomenon.

The second was chronic fatigue. Even though I slept good from the night before, I was tired all the time. Every afternoon, I was ready for a nap. And I never napped. Since I could not afford for this happening at work, I started drinking coffee in the afternoon. Something I never did before. My biggest hurdle, the only way to get coffee, I had to go to our breakroom. And our breakroom was on the main floor towards the back of the dispatcher's room. Meaning I would be away from my desk for 3-4 minutes. And drinking coffee meant more bathroom trips like every hour on the hour. My trips to the breakroom and the bathroom did not go unnoticed. I thought I had side effects from the new and expensive medication from my neurologist. My six-month appointment was in early February and I will talk to him about this medication.

Nothing had changed the day of my Neurologist appointment. I told him about the same issues, including the new symptoms. The increase in headaches, fatigue, and the partial eye blockages. I challenged him, asked if I had a drug interaction with his medicine of choice. Before I knew it, he is telling me it sounds like I am having seizures. Seizures? I had not had any bouts of unconsciousness with my ongoing health. How could he come to this conclusion? Would any testing reveal my abnormalities? There would be no convincing him. No matter what I said, his mind was made up. He increased my medication to 900#mg. The worst thing of all, he would not sign off on my DMV paperwork. My driver's license would be suspended for six months. Now, what am I going to do?

License or not, I kept driving. I did not have any other options. I certainly did not want to tell my employer, as I had enough to worry about. No use adding fuel to the fire, as I had enough stress with repeating the same mistakes. All the retraining, no matter how many times we went over things, the errors continued. My confidence was fading fast.

I was exactly one week shy before my six-month Neurologist appointment. Left for work and like any other morning, it was still dark. As I left Marshall, a police car pulled me over as one of my headlights did not work. Oh no, I am in big trouble! He ran my license and appeared suspended. He wrote me a sizable ticket, which included a loss in points (3-4). What am I going to do? How am I going to get the car back to our house? How am I going to get to and from work? As fate would have it, one of my neighbors worked a few miles from my employer. She would get me to and from work until I get my licenses back. Lovely. Time to wait until they set a date for my court case/hearing.

On August 8, my neurologist appointment went by with no issues. He asked how I was feeling. I told him I am fine. I lied to him once again. But I learned from my earlier appointments. Decided it was best to keep my mouth shut. All I wanted from him was to sign my DMV paperwork. Once he did, I made my six-month appointment and got out of there.

In a few months, my court case/hearing arrived. On the day of my hearing, all I thought about was the amount of money to pay off the ticket. And how our auto insurance rate will skyrocket. As I arrived for court, I sat along a row of chairs until my name to be called. There must have been a dozen people in the room, including the judge and the administrative assistant. As I witnessed those ahead of me talk to the judge, I could sense he wanted people to be direct and to the point. Listening intently to the sincerity of your voice. Do you feel remorse for your actions? I know I did.

Finally, the administrative assistant called me. She asked how I wanted to plea towards the charges against me. I pleaded no contest. No use fighting it, as I know what I did was wrong. Moments later, I am sitting across from the judge. He asks me to explain what happened. He asked me why I drove with a suspended license. I explained I had no choice. I did not know anyone who could go back and forth from work. Taking a taxi or any car aid services was too expensive, $200 per week. I gave him my DMV paperwork that was signed one week after they pulled over me. I told him I was sorry and that I accept the consequences. The Judge looked at me, in deep thought, and told me he is throwing the ticket out. He warned me to never appear before him again. I thanked him, walked out to my vehicle, and nearly passed out due to the stress. With a deep breath, I thanked my lucky stars, and headed for home.

At the beginning of October, they placed me on blood pressure medication (They changed a few times/types of beta-blockers) and Lipitor (Atorvastatin) to lower my cholesterol. Lower my cholesterol? Why? I ate a healthy diet that was low in cholesterol. I worked out and was in good shape. I did not want more medication that could screw up my INR levels.

Time for my year-end review was fast approaching, and I hoped for better results. No good news as I continued making costly errors. The same errors from the previous year. My supervisor talked about my attendance and how I was calling in sick. And my time management issue came up again—all my coffee runs, my trips to the bathroom. Frustrating. Why was I still making the same mistakes? Now I am worried about my job security.

Around this time, I noticed I was having what I would call a "Frozen Speech (Apraxia)." I knew what I wanted to say but could not. There would be nothing for 5-10 seconds. Customers that were on the phone during my frozen speech episodes would ask, "Hello, are you still there?" I would tell the customer any excuse that came to mind. Something like we must have had a minor glitch in the phone line. Any excuse to avoid losing the customer.

On April 7th, 2010, the day for my Stress Test. I could save them the time. Yes, I am stressed. It was time to evaluate out my heart while walking or running on a treadmill. The Cardio Stress Test was interesting. Only by using electrodes and a treadmill will they watch my hearts' ability to respond to external stress. I prepared accordingly.

First thing after I arrived, I changed into my exercising clothing and my shoes that I only use on the treadmill. Next, they tell me how the test using various speeds and inclines. The time would be approx. 15-20 minutes, which depended upon if I could finish the test. During the test, they would ask me the level of difficulty, using a one-to-ten scale. It did not concern me about the test's length, as I usually walk on my treadmill for 30-40 minutes. The inclined part was something I avoided. I did not see the benefit other than unwanted stress to my knees.

The test starts. The first five minutes were easy. The speeds were minimal, nowhere near the speed I used to warm-up. As time passed, the speed and inclines increased. With every passing minute, the speed and incline got faster and higher. Just envision the actor Dolph Lundgren in the movie "Rocky 4". His character, Ivan Drago, was running on the treadmill for his fight preparation. Different speeds and inclines to make you want to fall or quit. Whatever came first.

After ten minutes or longer, I was annoyed answering their questions, "How would rate the level of difficulty"? I am tired, sweating like a pig, out of breath, and they want me to tell them a number? The thoughts and feelings that ran through my head. I wanted to yell out, "What do you think? My legs are ready to fall off, and my heart is ready to explode. Don't you see my heart levels on the computer you are using? Please, look at those numbers. It's ten, ok!" But I did not say anything as I was out of breath and wished to stay out of trouble. I am proud to say I made it to the end without stopping. But it took a couple of days to recover.

In the Fall of 2010, I had what would be my last appointment with my current neurologist. He was as cold and distant as usual. Nor did he seem interested in helping me. Kept my mouth shut the entire time as I wanted nothing to do with him. Why talk as he never listened. As I left, I knew it was time for a change. Find a neurologist who would make the time, to listen and take me seriously. One quick phone call and a change in neurologists was made.

My ongoing issues at work continued. There was no light at the end of the tunnel. I could not break free from making the same mistakes repeatedly. My job performance review that October was abysmal, as I expected. I was given a written warning due to my performance. I was digging a hole so deep that I may never climb out from. My thoughts were so focused on job security that I lost out on my family life. I barely remember anything. My life was spiraling out of control before my very eyes, yet I did not seem to notice. There was nothing that I felt inside of me as I was no longer enjoying life.

2011 started much like the last couple of years. The never-ending issues at work. The amounts of stress that continued to build. No longer thinking clearly, regardless of whether I was at home or work, or somewhere in-between. I was not thinking clearly as my mind was focused on other aspects in my life.

I was constantly thinking about driving and my lack of focus behind the wheel. Questioning myself. What if I got into an accident? What if I hurt others? I did not want to take the chance and decided it would be best if I stopped. I informed my human resource manager of my decision to stop driving. And explained to him that I had two neighbors that would drive me to and from work. He thanked me and said that being upfront with him took courage.

I was calling in sick often due to my fatigue. The fatigue was terrible. I was wiped out for days on end, sleep most of the day. In the process, I burnt all my paid time off by the end of March. At the same time, I received another written warning due to my performance and attendance. On April 28, I ended up suffering a panic attack at work. I was taken to the ER by our human resources manager, who told me I was in and out of it throughout the drive. I do not recall checking in, how I got to the room or anything that happened. There was no one around when I came to. It was not long before a doctor appeared. It was here when I first heard the words, "chronic fatigue" ever used. The doctor stressed how vital discussing the chronic fatigue upon my June 23rd Neurologist appointment. I do not remember much else other than Laurie driving me home.

All my worries about losing my job came to fruition. On the afternoon of May 12, 2011, the company's human resource manager called me to the conference room. In the room was the company's sales manager, with whom I had a good relationship. We talked about how I already had fourteen mistakes so far in the year, costing the company customers and money. After learning about my mistakes and money lost, I was fired. It meant failure.

As the conversation continued, we went over paperwork consisting of the company's insurance plan with Short-Term and Long-Term Disability. Deep down, they knew something was wrong with me. They gave me more chances than I deserved. And now they were offering help after my employment. I was glad they were willing to help with disability, but it does not change the fact that I was no longer with the company. I boxed up my personal belongings, said my goodbyes, and left. Now what am I going to do?

FIVE

Somebody get me a Doctor

"Isn't it a bit unnerving that doctors
call what they do "practice"?"
Comedian George Carlin

So much for my future, like a stable job. Stable health. Stable doctors I can trust. The quote will shape as this Chapter gets rolling when doctors' and clinics' focus keeps growing. You will come across paragraphs upon paragraphs of summaries from the various Doctors/Specialists I have visited. Be prepared as I typed their writings verbatim, as there was no way I could replace them into my own words. And there was no way I would shorten their summaries. Keeping their notes intact would prove useful towards all the different views doctors, mostly specialists, had of me.

I will always be grateful for my former employer as they offered me disability insurance. Knowing that I had Disability Insurance, I knew we would receive money every week. I started the process of Social Security Disability Insurance (SSDI). Thank God I could complete all the paperwork online. I did not know what I was getting myself into. Was I putting the cart in front of the horse? I did not believe we had a precise diagnosis for my health issues. Epilepsy. I was seizure free for four years. Yet, the problems remained. Now I have a new Neurologist (#3) and an appointment within a month. There are answers on the horizon.

My neurologist appointment went better than I expected. I did not set the bar too high. We were still in the same clinic/area as my former neurologist (2#). She took the time to ask me questions when specific issues happened. What was my status concerning seizure-like activities? She took a firm approach concerning my dizzy spells. First, she lowered my Lamictal levels by 200#mg (900 to 700). Second, she scheduled a four-night hospital stay to perform a Video EEG starting just days after our appointment. Whoa. She was a breath of fresh air.

After four long days of suffering through boredom, aided trips to the bathroom, and eating bland hospital food, it was time to go home. As they were taking off the electrodes, I could feel the rubber pieces left behind. I knew I would spend extra time in the shower, pulling off the rubber pieces when I washed my hair. However, I would be at home. The thought of going home brought a massive smile to my face. As fate would have it, I had a blurry vision episode just minutes from my house. Why couldn't that have happened while at the hospital, hooked up to the electrodes? Great.

My time home gave me a chance to get things back to some sort of normality. Like being around my family, including my cat, Thomas. Throughout the entire year, Thomas watched me like he was my guardian angel. Wherever I went, he was shortly behind me. When I laid down, no matter if it waw our bed or on the couch, Thomas would curl up with me. He rarely left my side throughout the years. Like Blue, Thomas was a loyal cat. Who says that a dog is a man's best friend?

It was a difficult period with the kids. They were home from school on Summer Break. I had my moments when I felt good and moments, I felt awful. I do not recall how things went that Summer, other than going camping. Whatever we did during that time would require me to look at photos from that Summer. Other than that, I have absolutely no memory of anything else. Nothing. That is pathetic.

I was looking forward to my follow-up Neurologist appointment on July 21. I always thought about what did the Video EEG reveal. Will we have some explanation for my issues? I was impatient. I wanted the answers. The time came, and I was disappointed. They found a couple of minor tremors, nothing worthwhile to make any assessment. The next step would be an MRI of my head/brain, scheduled for the following day.

I had no idea what an MRI (Mechanical Resonance Image) would consist of. As I walked into the room and got an opportunity to see the big ass machine that I would be going into, I panicked. I was not sure whether I was claustrophobic or not. But I knew we would find out soon, so I took my time walking over to the machine. As I laid down, they strap you in to keep you from moving around while inside. You will receive a set of headphones for wearing as it a little noisy inside. When everybody is ready, the platform you are laying on will take you inside the machine. You are stuck within the small confines of the inner part of the device. If you decide to keep your eyes open, you can watch the wheel spin around throughout the test. I would not if I were you. Personally, if I kept my eyes open, I would vomit. And being in a tight area, where would the vomit go? My eyes stayed shut. Thank God for the headphones. A little noisy? Were talking about as loud as my first rock concert! I was beyond relieved when the test was over. I could not get off the platform fast enough. All I wanted was to get out of there and never look back.

I received good news on October 12. Thankfully, my Long-Term Disability insurance was approved. The approval would give me a more extended period of coverage than Short Term would provide. Days later, as I talked with a Customer Service Representative with the disability insurance company, she asked me if I would like to speak to a lawyer concerning my SSDI. She explained that the group worked as a third party (Let us call them SCORS as I want to avoid using their real name). I thought that is a great idea. Who better to help get me off Long-Term Disability and onto SSDI than the insurance company? That proved to be a horrible decision.

I certainly had my hands full the latter part of 2011 into 2012. I was getting bombarded with emails and phone calls from SCORS. They were collecting information concerning my tests to my testimony. Things around the house were crazy, and family life was far from perfect. However, we knew we were moving in the right direction. We needed to be patient as things will not happen overnight. Remember the phrase, Rome was not built in a day.

March 2012

On March 22, I received an upsetting letter from my disability insurance company. As of April 1, they would be stopping my disability. Written within my letter, it says, "No medical correlation between accounting for the patient's complaints to 'be' unable to remain competitive in the workforce." I would later find out that the information was coming from my Neurologist #3. What is going on? What did she tell them? She has no idea how I live my life daily.

I was livid. Immediately, I was on the phone calling my Neurologist. I was fuming and ready to bite the head off from the first person who answers. It was a good thing I was on hold as the time gave me a chance to calm down. I would not chew out the nurses. It is not their fault. I told them what the disability insurance company had written, saying "No medical correlation to account for the patient's complaints to 'be' unable to remain competitive in the workforce" in my letter and how I hoped to get some clarification from my Neurologist. The nurse said she would talk to the Doctor and call me back as soon as possible. She was true to her word.

My Neurologist's nurse called me shortly after lunchtime. She explained that the insurance company asked my Neurologist direct questions concerning my condition. Half the questions needed a simple "Yes" or "No" answer (I would get a copy of the questionnaire at my next appointment). According to my Neurologist's findings, there was not enough information to support the continuation of disability benefits. In the disability company's eyes, I could return to the workforce with no limitations.

Towards the end of our conversation, the nurse mentioned that I should research APS, read over their website, and contact them. That is odd. Why would the nurse be telling me this? She worked for the entire Neurology Clinic. She did not work for one specific Doctor. Did she know someone that has APS? But how could she know my whole medical history and offer this advice? It made little sense. However, I followed the nurse's advice, which turned my entire world upside down!

I went and sat down at our computer desk to look up the APS website, www.apsfa.org. As I started reading the website and reviewing the symptoms, I almost fell out of my chair. I was going down the list, finding one health condition after another that I had. I honestly could not believe what I was reading. With Laurie's help, we called the Foundation. We talked to Christina "Tina" Pohlman. Tina was the current President, Executive Director, Co-Founder & Lupus/APS (Antiphospholipid Antibody Syndrome) Patient with a BS in Public Health Education of the APS Foundation of America, Inc. Tina was by far one of the most knowledgeable persons concerning APS.

What a conversation that turned out to be! She supplied the help that I desperately needed. Thank God Laurie was on the other phone. Tina asked thorough and detailed questions, some I could not answer correctly. I would easily forget and have trouble recalling things. Laurie discussed my inability to perform daily activities, limiting my long-distance driving, and my inability to balance our checkbook. I would turn the numbers around as I reviewed the bank statement. Laurie explained how she had to repeat things and use a dry erasable board to prevent me from forgetting. Times when I have left the stove/oven on. And how the simplest of tasks was becoming problematic and too much for me to manage. I needed help, and Tina was the answer.

We discussed my complete health history. We talked about my Doctors, including the locations of the Hospitals and Clinics. Tina mentioned that she has heard from several people who attended the same Hospital/Clinics and had similar adverse outcomes. She strongly urged that I come to LaCrosse to the Gundersen Lutheran Medical Center. Tina was a current patient and knew the specialists that she wanted me to see. It was a suggestion that I took to heart and decided to move forward.

Tina started making appointments with the Doctors that she felt were critical to see. The first and clearly the most important would be a Hematologist. A Hematologist is a Doctor who specializes in researching, diagnosing, treating, and preventing blood disorders and disorders of the lymphatic system (lymph nodes and vessels). After setting up my appointment, she called me with the Doctor's appointment date and time, late morning on July 3, 2012. The Hematologist wanted my medical records released and sent to Gundersen as soon as possible. That proved problematic as they arrived late.

By moving forward, we needed to start planning for the medical bills. I would not be bringing in any income. How are we going to pay for all of this? We are up to our eyebrows in medical bills. Laurie was working two jobs, often six to seven days a week. I remember twenty straight days. She was the only person who was bringing in any money and health benefits whatsoever. Money was tight. We cashed in our retirement savings and mutual funds, accepting that we will be losing money for early withdrawal and taxes. We used our credit card. We did whatever we could to save money to help with bills.

In my discussions with Tina, we felt that it was time to talk to a lawyer to gather information on how we could manage the wrongful termination of my long-term disability benefits. Could I sue them? Do I have a case? Am I nuts to sue them while I was dealing with my SSDI case at the same time? Through a close friend, she recommended that I talk to a specific lawyer group, (Let us call them Lincoln Hawk, S.C.) as they were great working for ex-employees against insurance companies. After a couple of phone calls and a mailed envelope full of paperwork, the law firm decided that I had a case and asked if I wanted to move forward with a wrongful claim lawsuit against the insurance company. I said yes. On April

12, I signed the paperwork agreeing to the case. In time, it would prove that I made the right decision. Little would happen over two years as the negotiations to avoid court takes time. Within that time, you ended up forgetting about it as there would be little to no news.

Due to disability benefits and income loss cancellation, I started siphoning or cutting back on my Lamictal medication. They were too expensive, becoming the obvious choice to begin with. Instead of 900#mg, I was down to 600#mg. "I believe" I tried 500#mg for a while, but I cannot remember if this was true. I did not dare to cut back on the rest of my medication, especially medications like my blood thinners and those for my heart. Siphoning those would be a considerable gamble, something I was not going to take any chances on. I will pay whatever the cost.

It a month, I was in constant communication with my Primary Care Physician. I discussed in great length the possibility of having APS. We talked about all the symptoms I was having and how similar they were with APS. After reviewing the APS website, she agreed to send me to a Hematologist. I scheduled an appointment with an affiliated Hematologist in LaCrosse. I remember being told not to worry about the title of the clinic, Oncology (Cancer). Awesome. Thank you, Dr. Harris!

As with any other doctor appointment, they started as expected, with a nurse to take all my vitals. She was polite and asked me a fair number of questions concerning my related symptoms. I felt relaxed talking with her. When she left the room, I had an overall feeling that I was at the right clinic. That would change when the doctor walked in. Our discussion was odd, surprisingly essential for a specialist, and dare if I say, going through the motions while discussing my symptoms. When he talked, it felt like he was telling me exactly what I wanted to hear. Unknown to me, there are specific tests that are needed to confirm an APS diagnosis. Surprisingly, the doctor did not order labs. However, he said after reviewing my medical file, and he agreed that I had APS.

Once he confirmed APS, I asked him about ordering a Neuro-Psych evaluation. I explained how crucial this test would be to accurately measure my skill levels and brain function—information vital concerning my disability. I further explained how APS could have similar symptoms like Multiple Sclerosis and other brain infirmities. But he was the only one that had the authority to order one. My Primary Care Physician did not. He said he would draft a report confirming his APS diagnosis, recommend a Neuro-Psych test, and send it to my PCP. He finished continuing the same action as blood thinners and regular (scheduled) coagulation testing (INR). And with that, he got up and left. I thought that was easy. As I walked out the door, all I could think of that I was positive for APS. Two different Doctors with an APS diagnosis.

A week after my Hematology appointment, my PCP received his report. To her surprise, there was no recommendation to perform a Neuro-Psych test. If he felt I had APS, then why would he not evaluate my skills. My PCP appointment centered around the lack of concern he felt towards ordering the Neuro-Psych test. She questioned how he could be sure that I had APS without one. I could sense during our conversation that she was taken aback by the tone of her voice. She said she was sorry that she could not do more for me. I thanked her and walked out the door to my vehicle. All I wanted to do was call the Hematologist's office and asked him, "Why are you doing this? You tell me that a Neuro-Psych evaluation was needed and then told my PCP that a Neuro-Psych test isn't?" Now I am screwed from having a Neuro-Psych test without his recommendation.

April 2012

Starting in April, I started seeing a psychiatrist. I was stressed out, feeling depressed, and desperate for help. I was not happy, snapping at people. I was jealous of families who could take big vacations, brag about it, and plaster pictures all over social media. I could not relax. My state of mind was preoccupied with my disability findings and my family's lack of money. My first psychiatrist appointment sucked. We barely made it ten minutes, and at once he wanted to amend my meds. No, no, no. Back the train up to the station. Making immediate changes to my medication before checking with my PCP could be dangerous. Dare I say life-threatening. The psychiatrist was nice enough to type "Refused a change in medication" in his notes for all to see, like Disability Insurance companies. We made it through a couple of appointments to assess my mental wellbeing. He felt that I was suffering from a decrease in cognitive skills and problem-solving. Yet, when I asked him about a Neuro-Psych evaluation, I was told I did not need it. In just three sessions, he found that I would be ok to return to the workforce on a full-time basis. I requested to see someone else within their office to be reevaluated. With that, he gave me a referral and said the office would call me.

I was referred to a Licensed Clinical Social Worker to discuss my past and present challenges that my family and I are enduring. Our first session was encouraging as she was curious and compassionate to my feelings. Soon I found myself in a familiar place. She never assessed any of my skills or lack thereof. It was not long before she felt I was better off seeing someone else for extra help concerning my health issues. She told me she was limited in how to improve my mindset and skills. So, she referred me back to my original Psychiatrist. No way that was going to happen. All I was asking for was their help and that place did just the opposite. Thank you for increasing both my anxiety and depression levels; I felt emotionally lost and unappreciated. What a waste of money.

June 2012

Allen Cognitive Levels of Function testing took place on the fifth. The test, administered by an Occupational Therapist unaffiliated with my current Doctors, hospital, or clinics. My test results found I was at a Level 5 with mild functional decline, beginning deficits in abstract thought processes. As listed word for word listed under Level 5. "Person begins to have difficulty using complex information. The problems observed were with memory, judgment, reasoning, and planning." She noticed minor problems within our conversation. "Difficulties with the performance of complex daily tasks include reading, writing, calculating, managing finances, job performance, driving, meal preparation, shopping, or following a complex medication schedule—concrete tasks such as dressing, grooming, and bathing as usual. Hazardous activities may need monitoring for safe performance. Self-centered behavior or the inability to consider the needs of others is common as the person loses sight of the larger picture."

July 3, 2012

Finally, the day had arrived. My first appointment at Gundersen Lutheran Medical Center. To drive two-and-a-half hours away. Most were all interstate driving, saving time and gas money. Having my music blasting helped to make the drive tolerable.

I checked in and went to the floor that housed the Hematology/Oncology Clinic. It was here when I finally met Tina. Now I had a face to the name. Tina was all business and does not tolerate ineffective doctors. She was steps ahead for what I needed for tests, doctors, or anything of which you could think. Amazing. She would be more than just an APS Advocate, a great friend, and someone I would trust my life with. My appointment with the Hematologist did not go as planned because of my medical records not arriving on time. I had blood drawn for labs. But the doctor had nothing to match them up without my records. Honestly, it did not matter, as my levels were high for APS. Weirdly, the APS diagnosis came across as good news. At least I knew at this point that I was getting the correct diagnosis. That coming here was the right thing. And now we had proof that Epilepsy was not to blame for my health issues.

On the 13th, I would be back at Gundersen to meet with a Doctor in Neuroscience, which is simply the nervous system's scientific study. Focus on the brain and its impact on behavior and cognitive functions. My first assessment to help to figure out my cognitive skills. The complete summary is:

"According to Mr. Radke and his records, the first blood clots were discovered in 2000, for which he underwent treatment. Over time, he had been diagnosed with lupus anticoagulant blood disorder. More recently, he is being assessed for antiphospholipid antibody syndrome, which is also an autoimmune clotting disorder. He continues under treatment for this. Towards the end of 2006 and into 2007, he had three tonic-clonic seizures. He is currently on Lamictal for this as well. No other tonic-clonic seizures have been noted. There has been concern about the possibility of absence seizures. He apparently has had numerous episodes where he has become unresponsive for a few minutes at a time with loss of memory for these events."

The summary further states, "He does experience increased fatigue afterwards. Frequency of these may fluctuate, although, typically tend to be at least once or twice a day. He also indicates that since 2000, he will experience episodes of partial blindness in his left eye. This will occur at random times and last for a couple minutes. Again, he will have some fatigue afterwards, although, has awareness of the event. This can happen from a couple times a week to once or twice a day."

"He also reports that since 2000, with this being worse after 2007, having episodes of Deja vu, and at times odd feelings, as if he is somewhat separated from his body. These again last only a few minutes at a time. These experiences also vary in frequency as well. He also reports spells of "dizziness." This can occur sitting or standing. These also can occur at different times, and last for only a few minutes each time."

"He also reports that over the past few years, he has become increasingly sensitive to smell. Any sort of strong odor will create strong nausea and dizziness. This can also trigger headaches as well. He does indicate that beyond headaches, he does have severe migraines. These will often occur in the morning and will lead to significant fatigue the rest of the day. These have been occurring a couple times a month and have become particularly noticeable over the past year."

"Since his tonic-clonic seizure, he has experienced increasing difficulties with memory and attention. These have become particularly worse since 2010. Previously, he had apparently worked quite successfully as a manager in business. This was verified in a written report from his wife. In fact, in 2009, he did manage to complete an associate degree in Management with a 3.6GPA (Please note – It should be 3.86, not 3.6GPA). However, has noted since then that memory and concentration is getting worse. It is to the point he is extremely absent-minded and cannot keep track of even a few details at a time. He has left the stove on, has transposed numbers, and forgotten what he has been told, even just a few moments ago."

The summary continues, "Over the past couple years, he has also noted some trembling of the hands. This started in the right hand, but now at times will affect the left hand. This also tends to come and go as well. He also on occasion will have facial twitching and nystagmus. Mr. Radke reports that he does have a premorbid history of mild dysphoria, and he tends to be a somewhat high-strung individual. However, this did not previously interfere with functioning. Over the past few years, his anxiety and depression has increased. He does experience recurring panic attacks, in which he has racing heart, and a vague feeling of dread. He is currently on fluoxetine and clonazepam for this."

"Mr. Radke did produce a neuropsychological report conducted in September 2011. This report had indicated a video EEG had indicated no clear etiology for the reported symptoms. However, the report also indicated that a recent "head MRI revealed a 3 mm x 2 mm T2-hyperintense cyst within the left parietal fissure. This results in mild mass effect on left hippocampal function." (Please note that I had no idea or informed that I had a cyst). There was no further description of how this might play into his symptoms. Neuro psych testing did indicate some overall cognitive slowing. However, this was attributed to a learning disorder, even though the patient had no prior documented learning disability. Mr. Radke has been feeling frustrated with what he perceives is lack of answers and guidance from his current Doctors/Clinics. Therefore, he is coming to Gundersen Lutheran for second opinion. He is being seen in Neuropsychology for an outpatient assessment of cognition.

He has also been scheduled for an evaluation with Neurologist #4. A complete Neuropsychology Assessment testing will take place on July 24 of 2012." Geez, I have an issue or two. What is in store for me at my next appointment?

July 24, 2012

Doctor appointments with an Ophthalmologist and a Neuroscientist for Neuropsychic Assessment testing. My appointment with the Ophthalmologist was the same as a regular eye appointment. We needed to find out why I was having trouble with a partial loss of vision. Here are his notes from my appointment:

"This the first time he has been seen. Patient does have quite a complex medical history. He has been diagnosed with Epilepsy in the past. Now they call his medical syndrome APS. Patient has for the last two years had a period where part of his vision in his left eye will go black. It will last for three to five minutes and then goes away. He feels like he has had that happen two to three times in the last three months. Potential amaurosis fugax (Amaurosis fugax is a condition in which a person cannot see out of one or both eyes due to a lack of blood flow to the eye(s). The condition is a symptom of an underlying problem, such as a blood clot or insufficient blood flow to the blood vessels that supply the eye. Other names for amaurosis fugax include transient monocular blindness, transient monocular visual loss, or temporary visual loss). As a result, I did contact neurology. He is scheduled to see Neurologist #4. I explained to her his symptoms. She will review his chart and possibly move his appointment up. In addition, I did go over stroke-like symptoms with the patient. I told him if he had any symptoms like that, that he should go to the emergency room right away."

Now it was time to get my Neuroscience appointment. Since my Ophthalmologist ran late, I had to haul ass as I would not be late or miss my Neuro-Psych evaluation. I did not want to screw this up. Yet, I ended up being 15 minutes late. At least they were ready and waiting for me. I was a little stressed (anxious) when I got here. Did not have a lunch. Yet, I was pumped and ready to go through with the testing. The testing ended up taking 210 minutes, which went over the allotted time. Oops. My bad. She would write:

"The assessment is indicating cognitive slowing and diminished attention capacity. This could certainly be the effect of the anticonvulsant medications. There is also though the finding of severely impaired ability to maintain alertness and focus over time. This is at a level greater than expected from solely the medication. This certainly could come from a combination of chronic medical condition affecting general function of the brain along with the chronic effects of severe anxiety. He is, however, also showing focal deficits (Impairments of nerve, spinal cord or brain function) in certain aspects of language, as well as visual spatial facial perception (Short term memory, facial & emotional perceptions) which would be more specific to medial/anterior temporal lobe function (Visual memories, processing sensory input, language recognition, new memories, focal seizures)."

"Mr. Radke's performance on MMPI-2 (Minnesota Multiphasic Personality Inventory) plus other aspects of his reporting do also indicate though that he is likely experiencing a severe anxiety reaction to his ongoing medical condition. This extreme anxiety reaction can result in increased preoccupation and focus on minute physical and cognitive functioning which in turn could exacerbate several symptoms he is already experiencing. Mr. Radke's MMPI-2 (MMPI-RF) profile indicates a likely premorbid history of being high strung with the tendency towards a greater attention to detail. The profile does reflect that he is likely experiencing extreme significant stressors such as a medical condition. As a result, he had severely elevated anxiety and mood disturbances. This does include excessive preoccupation with even minute physical symptoms and a general feeling of incapacity and helplessness."

"Mr. Radke will be undergoing further neurological evaluation with Neurologist #4 to clarify the neurological basis of his complaints. To be clear, the results from neuropsychological assessment do not indicate a factitious disorder nor somatoform disorder. However, it does indicate a severe anxiety reaction which can be complicating treatment and stabilization of medical condition. Therefore, consideration should also be given to obtain better control of anxiety reaction process, preferably in ways that would, of course, not lower the seizure threshold." Ouch. That was harsh.

I continued to pursue a Neuro-Psych evaluation closer to home, beyond my Neuro-Psych evaluation. A backup plan, having a second opinion. I had been searching for months and had nothing. Trying to find an opportunity was next to impossible. I even contacted the State of Wisconsin's Division of Vocational Rehabilitation (DVR). I had a one and one meeting with a Vocational Rehabilitation Counselor. The Counselor wrote to me, dated August 7, the following concerning notes from Neurologist #4 at Gundersen. "I did receive the records from Gundersen Clinic this morning. However, they do not appear to contain the information I need, a final report from Neurologist #4. A diagnostic impression from the psychometrist and a note that you would be further evaluated by Neurologist #4. However, there is no actual diagnosis or clear report about functioning based on your test results (Please note - She received the Psychological testing by computer dated July 13 from the last paragraph). To clarify, I do not need all the individual test results. I am not able to interpret those. The examining psychologist does that in the report, which is the document I need (Please note – The examining psychologist's report does not exist or released by the Wisconsin DVR). The current documentation also doesn't confirm the diagnosis of APS which you've discussed."

I was puzzled and confused by the notes she listed. Her determination from the one-on-one meeting took 30 minutes in length. No labs or records were asked. How she came to this final summary is baffling, and she comes across like I (we) are wasting her time that the state will not offer any help. What a waste of time!! Her findings or report proves my point that no one from the area was interested in helping me. My Neuro-Psych Assessment from Gundersen would be all I needed. What I could not understand was why was this test so hard to get scheduled or performed?

September 17, 2012

Appointment #1 – Rheumatology

What a long day! Nor was it a great day. I am back at Gundersen Lutheran Medical Center. Thank God my Mother made the trip with me. Other than Tina, my Mom was my rock throughout my travels to and from LaCrosse. Tina planned for us to stay at The Asbury Hospitality House, an overnight stay for patients and their families. It was a house that could house four families at a time. It was like a regular house with a full kitchen of supplies, minus food. All they asked for was a $10 donation for the one-night stay. The place came in handy on many occasions. It was what I needed to get a good night's rest as I got tired quickly and knew I had a long day ahead of me.

I had labs drawn to start the morning before my day's appointments. They were needed for my first appointment, beginning with a Rheumatologist for the first time. My appointment with him led to my Systemic Lupus Erythematosus diagnosis. Lupus is one of many disorders of the immune system known as autoimmune diseases. In autoimmune diseases, the immune system turns against parts of the body it is designed to protect. This leads to inflammation and damage to various body tissues. Lupus can affect many parts of the body, including the joints, skin, kidneys, heart, lungs, blood vessels, and brain. Although people with the disease may have many different symptoms, some of the most common ones include extreme fatigue, painful or swollen joints (arthritis), unexplained fever, skin rashes, and kidney problems. My situation was pointing more to NPSLE, also known as CNS Lupus, as all my labs were off the charts. All right. Good news per se. Exactly how I wanted to start this day off. Bring on my Hematologist.

My appointment went as planned without any problems or new issues. It was a review of things we have already discussed, most notably the APS diagnosis. Now we needed to add the Systemic Lupus Erythematous to the mix. Even though our talk was brief, the

SLE diagnosis would take a while to sink in. I did not have a grasp of Lupus. That would later come in forms of literature (pamphlets) that Tina carried with her. Thank God for them, as I learned about the different forms of Lupus, the aftereffects on the body.

Appointment #2 – Psychiatry

The next appointment would be with a Psychiatrist. Once again, I was not comfortable with the overall experience I received before attending Gundersen. Talking with Tina, we felt it would be best to see a Psychiatrist as this could shed light on problems that earlier Doctors overlooked. While I was waiting to see the doctor, I had a partial loss of vision in my right eye. Odd as partial loss of vision usually happens in my left eye. Tina at once called my Hematologist's nurse for advice. The doctor at once instructed me to take a chewable baby aspirin, and if my vision did not clear up, I would be off to the Emergency Room for evaluation. This episode lasted for only a couple of minutes. The good news was the baby aspirin worked and still does today. Once things with my vision returned to normal, fatigue started to settle in.

I spent an hour talking to the Psychiatrist. We started with first assessments and then on to my thoughts, feelings, etc. End up with questions, such as do I feel stable or do I wish to harm myself. Yes doctor, I am going off the rails on a crazy train. I made a few jokes, concerning being a father for example. She laughed as she knew it was all in good humor. She wrote the following integrative summary:

"The patient is a 40-year-old male who presents with concerns about his health and a desire to approach his problems by learning how to deal with them and not relying on medication alone. He reports that his Psychiatrist sees him once every six weeks and focuses more on medications. He has seen a counselor about three times but felt she was also more medication focused. He came to this facility on the recommendation of another patient who has the same autoimmune diagnosis and recommended this facility, including Behavioral Health. He would like to learn how to cope with his health problems and his worry better. He also wants to manage his depressive symptoms better."

"We did talk about the reality that he lives two-and-a-half hours away and that he would probably not be able to afford coming on a regular basis for therapy. We talked about finding a referral for him that would be closer home. However, he did agree to come back in about a month, giving me time to review his records and time to research where there may be a referral nearer to him in the Madison area. He does not sound as though he was very good at clarifying what he might have wanted from a counselor when he initially contacted one. We spent some time doing that today. He is a very proud man who would like to be self-reliant and feel some worth. He also is anxious and seems to have some obsessive-compulsive qualities as he noted he keeps track of his health issues on a spread sheet."

"He is struggling with worries about his health and the worthless feelings due to his inability to work at this time. His family is important to him, and there are times he has entertained thoughts of suicide, although he says he would not do it because his family would be hurt. The patient did not wish for his family to be directly involved in treatment at this time. The patient will return in about a month. At that time, we will come up with a treatment plan and probably a referral to someone closer to his home. Also, I will help him clarify exactly what he wants from a therapist, so he can set appropriate goals and be more assertive in requesting what it is he needs to feel more worthwhile, to manage his anxiety and to manage depressive symptoms." Another doctor appointment completed. Which doctor appointment is next?

Appointment #3 - Neurology

Time to meet neurologist #4. She was calm and easy to talk to. We talked about my dizzy spells, headaches, nausea, and cognitive decline. We went over my prior history with my other three Neurologists, what they found. She had me perform a few simplistic tests, which varied from the ones I have had done with earlier

Neurologists. One was holding my hands straight out and keep them there, "I believe" for ten to fifteen seconds. I did not understand why, nor did I ask. We went through a neurologic exam, speech, motor skills, sensory, coordination, and gait (walk). All would be normal.

She would write: "Mr. Radke has a seizure disorder which has been good control with Lamictal. The reduction in dose made one year ago has not been helpful and I doubt any of his symptoms are medication related. I recommend a repeat level on the lower dose. He has uncontrolled headaches, with migrainous features with the more severe episodes due to their frequent occurrence this would be best be managed with a daily medication. He also has uncontrolled anxiety so would recommend a medication which may help to address both problems such as Venlafaxine (Effexor)."

"The recurrent spells of vision loss are concerning. They have occurred despite a therapeutic INR without reported residual. They are not consistently associated with headaches and do not sound consistent with a migraine aura. Of greatest concern would be amaurosis fugax but this would seem unusual with the number of episodes and lack of any residual. The amaurosis fugax itself usually does not result in permanent disability. However, there is an increased risk for stroke. I recommend an evaluation in ophthalmology with Humphrey Visual Field testing. I also recommend a repeat MRI of the brain and MRA of the head and neck. The episodes of vertigo are also of unclear etiology but have been present for several years, are brief and not disabling. We will watch these for now."

Appointment #4 – Neuroscience

Finally, to end the day be with my Neuroscientist to discuss the complete results from my Neuropsychology Assessment appointment. What a revelation. I could not believe what we would be discussing. I must have read those results dozens of times and still have a rough time accepting the consequences. The tests revealed that I had a three milliliter by 2-milliliter cyst, the size of an eraser you would find on a number 2 pencil. Whoa. Excuse me, doctor, but back the train up to the station. My recent Neurologist (#3) did not mention anything concerning a cyst. If she did, I am 99.9% sure that I would have remembered. No further remark would be made by my former clinic report, including the entire evaluation of my functional capabilities.

I would find years later in the report that, "They were unable to pinpoint an etiology or give me a clear treatment plan." Why wouldn't someone tell me? It was not that important for me to know or worry over. We at once talked about my cyst. He informed me the size of the cyst and the hippocampus' function, of short and long-term memory. Without hesitation, I asked if surgery was a possibility for the cyst's removal. Unfortunately, surgery would do more harm than good. He showed me where the brain's temporal part was and how there would be no entry point to remove the cyst. So, is my cyst the good news or the bad news concerning the rest of my summary? I wanted to ask how long I have had this, but I already knew the answer we do not know. But it gave me a start to find the reasons why I was having trouble with my memory. I cannot help but wonder how long I have had Neurological issues. Do the findings explain prior erratic behaviors? Would it prove anything, or would the information be irrelevant? Here is the complete summary:

"Mr. Radke is experiencing severe or moderate impairment, low average, and demonstrating significant motor slowing and diminished bimanual coordination. His Verbal Comprehension Index rate was in the twenty-seven percentiles. A severe impairment of Sustained Attention/Inhibition. Moderate impairment at Speed of Processing. Mild impairment in the Ability to Prioritize. Low average score in both Problem Solving and Sequential Thought Process/Planning. He also demonstrated significantly impaired ability to maintain alertness and focus over time. For example, on the TOVA (Test of Variables of Attention), he had more errors of omission than 99.9% of the people his age. This indicates that this is not so much an issue of being distractible. Rather he is simply having trouble with maintaining alertness."

"He does show some rudimentary skills at organization with sequential thought process. However, because of the other impairments in speed and alertness, anything beyond a few details, he becomes quickly overwhelmed. Mr. Radke would be hard on himself at times, becoming upset when he did not know the answer or knew he had the answer incorrect but was able to persist. On the language measures, Mr. Radke is not simply demonstrating just diminished fluency, but he is also demonstrating diminished ability to even organize his thoughts into words. On language tasks from the WAIS-IV, those items that required only a brief response, he responded fairly well. Those that required more elaborate and organized response, he faired more poorly."

"The focal deficits instead of a generalized global impairment would indicate that he (Mr. Radke) did put forth full effort. Therefore, the results do not suggest that this is an individual who is motivated to present himself as impaired. In addition, the number of the symptoms he has mentioned, such as déjà vu and odd sensory stimuli, could potentially be seen in an individual with seizure activity in the temporal lobe regions. Furthermore, the findings regarding diminished language, fluency, diminished visual spatial functioning. Therefore, the assessment results would be consistent with the description of symptoms by Mr. Radke."

I love the following quotes, "Mr. Radke has been feeling frustrated with what he perceives is lack of answers and guidance from his current Doctors/Clinics. Therefore, he is coming to Gundersen Lutheran for second opinion." And "Therefore, the assessment results would be consistent with the description of symptoms by Mr. Radke." There you have it. All the Specialists at Gundersen agreed that I was suffering from chronic medical conditions APS and SLE. Yet, where I live, the clinics and hospitals that I placed my trust in found nothing wrong with me. They slapped on the Epilepsy diagnosis on me and acted like that was enough.

These are the disappointments I had to put up with for five long years. Outside of my Primary Care Physicians, no one did anything positive for me. Gundersen Lutheran Medical Center was able to find APS, Lupus, my cyst, and a thorough Neuropsychic Assessment testing with a full understanding of the loss of my cognitive skills.

Gundersen's overall findings contradict much if not most of the results written by my former Doctors/Clinics.

I did a lot of driving back and forth from LaCrosse/Onalaska. Overnight stays. Numerous tests. Numerous medical bills. Their billing department worked with Laurie and me to keep a monthly payment without busting our chops every couple of months. They understood we were living on one paycheck. I spent the next couple of years going to Gundersen. I did not trust making appointments with Specialists closer to home as they never took me seriously. They made my anxiety and depression issues worse. No way I wanted to come back to them.

As a family, we sacrificed a ton, mostly Laurie. We lived on her paycheck. She worked six days a week, at two or three different places. She traveled all over Southeastern Wisconsin to help facilities within their network that were short on PTA's. We did not do anything beyond camping as Laurie would be working. I was spending time and money traveling relentlessly in 2012. So much for creating fond memories with our children.

In the end, we did whatever it took to get answers finally. We listened and followed Tina's advice from start to finish. We got second opinions at Gundersen. I now have two precise diagnoses in APS & Lupus. Both considered disabilities. The questions of what was wrong with me disappeared. I no longer had guesswork or generic diagnoses. The newly confirmed diagnoses proved to be vital in both Disability cases. Time to move forward and get my disability approved.

SIX

The Struggle for Disability

"Concentrate on things your disability doesn't prevent you
from doing well and don't regret the things it interferes
with. Don't be disabled in spirit as well as physically."
Stephen Hawking (World Renown Theoretical Physicist)

I am a sports nut—especially football (Green Bay Packers!). I played a lot of sports throughout the years. Not anymore. My skills have diminished. And I am done. But as a fan, I watch and read about games/players, look at their stats, and often think about sports players who should call it quits. Why wait until you are a bench warmer due to low stats and a decline of skills. Look at the big picture. Only a few players are lucky enough to end their careers on top, winning a championship. Personal accolades, as being named Most Valuable Player (MVP). Or is it that burning desire to want more? As fans, we criticize players who have lost a step, slower, injury-prone, or declining skills. We ask ourselves, why are you still playing? Can't they recognize it is over? Time to walk away from the game.

Some players become expendable, as no one wants them. Prompting them to retire. Because of injuries, continuous rehabilitation, and losing the game's passion, it ends up taking a toll on a player. They must face the facts that their body will not let them continue doing their job. Unable to continue performing the way he once did. Reasons I like this story about former Indianapolis Colts Quarterback Andrew Luck. He played the entire 2016 season with an injury to his throwing shoulder. Once the 2016 season ended, he had surgery on his right shoulder, forcing him to miss the 2017 season.

The 2018 season turned out to be an outstanding year. They named Luck to his fourth Pro Bowl of his career and named the National Football League Comeback Player of the Year Award. Despite his success the prior year, Luck abruptly retired at the prime age of twenty-nine. On August 24, 2019, after seven seasons, Luck announced his retirement. At a press conference, he cited his recurrent cycle of injuries and rehabilitation as the primary reason, saying: "I have been stuck in this process. I have not been able to live the life I want to live. It has taken the joy out of this game. The only way forward for me is to remove myself from football. This is not an easy decision. It's the hardest decision of my life."

After reading about Andrew Luck, you understand why these sports players have a tough time walking away from the game they love. It is hard to admit you cannot do those things anymore!! Or you no longer have the proper mindset and skills you once had. You tell yourself that you are having a rough time. Give it a few days, and you will be better before you know it. But it does not get any better. There is a part of you that continues to think that you can do anything, that you are unstoppable, unbeatable. But deep down inside, you know better. You have reached the time in life when you must admit you cannot do it anymore. My body will not allow me to enjoy all the things I use to. It is easy to say it, but it is the most challenging thing to admit. You may feel like a failure, that you are letting people down. No matter how hard you try, that feeling never goes away.

I understand Andrew Luck. I would love to be in the workforce again. I want to be of value outside of my house, be around people, and talk to others. It is boring, being at home. It is like watching paint dry. I worry more. I have put on weight, much to my Cardiologists' dismay. I have become insecure, paranoid about what others may be thinking. Would they understand all the things I used to do, my accomplishments, before the health issues? It is a lifestyle change. I have an Associate Degree that has gone to waste. I did not get a chance to reach my full potential in the workforce or life. I am not trying to get everyone to feel sorry for me. Instead, I wish they could at least understand what I am going through, how my health can change as fast as turning on a light switch. You are a prisoner to your body. It does not get much simpler than that.

It is difficult to explain to anybody that I am disabled. You usually end up getting some weird looks. You do get those looks of disbelief. Or you are asked some bizarre questions. My favorite, "You don't look sick to me." I want to tell them that "You don't look like a Doctor to me." Would it help someone understand that my Central Nervous issues result from a car accident instead of an invisible chronic illness? Will they see or treat me differently? I have learned that sometimes it is best not to say anything. Think about this. What are your reasons that could sound like excuses to others? The chances are good that people will disappear from your life. They are nowhere to be found. Nowhere. No phone calls. No offers to help.

I had always kept Thomas Edison's quote to heart that "Many of life's failures are people who did not realize how close they were to success when they gave up." After my college degree, I expected to be successful in life. I would not accept anything less. Then my health changed. And I was not ready for this change to come, to be average or even one step below average! I did not want to accept the fact that I am no longer the person I was. I lost my dream to be successful. My only goal was to support better things for my family. Be able to take vacations without the thoughts of can we afford this? I lost my identity. There is a new Darren, something I do not like then nor today.

Making any plans can be difficult as I never know how I am going to feel. Sometimes you must be noncommittal. I tell those that If I am up to it, I will go. It is all I can do. I have been caught in a situation when we had plans to go to an amusement park close by where we live. On one occasion, when my children were younger, we picked a specific day when we were going to go. Both were excited. The night before, they were already talking about which rides they would be going on. I woke up the next morning, and I am lying down on the couch. I felt horrible. You name it, and I had it. Fatigue, joint pain, a headache that hurt so bad that I could not sleep. When my children saw me on the couch, they asked Laurie, "Does this mean we can't go to the amusement park today?" It just killed me inside. And it still sticks with me to this day about how I let them down.

The Social Security Disability process took forever. I had three SSDI hearings over three years. It was a grueling and stressful process. I understand that it needs to be to weed out those who may be faking or overstating their injuries/claims. People I know told me not to get my hopes up as they will usually deny your first claim, which they did. My claim never made it inside of a court/hearing room. Remember, I did not have a definite diagnosis at this point. I assumed it was Epilepsy. I was switching over to Long-Term Disability when the first claim was denied. I filed an appeal for a second hearing. That would end up taking 14 months. Sit and wait.

I signed on with SCORS (Please note-SCORS is not the company's actual name), the Short/Long-Term Disabilities Insurance third party for SSDI. I signed the paperwork on October 11 of 2011, my first opportunity to work with a law group. It would take until early December before they assigned me a lawyer. My lawyer sounded like a big shot type of lawyer when we spoke on the phone. Spewing out clichés like, I give you my word Mr. Radke that I will do whatever it takes to win your case. Spare me, Mr. lawyer man, I am sure you tell all your clients this. We traded phone calls and emails to give him and his staff all my health information to prepare for a second hearing. All the health information I had come from my local area's doctors/clinics. Once again, everything revolved around Epilepsy, as that was all we knew. So, we planned accordingly.

Everything would change by the end of September and early October 2012. Thanks to Gundersen Lutheran Medical Center, we had two diagnoses listed under disabled. The epilepsy diagnosis was dismissed by my doctors and replaced by APS & Lupus. I gave the

SCORS office that a change in diagnosis occurred, and I will send the recent information as it became available. As it did, I emailed everything to SCORS.

In the mail, I received my SSDI disability case date, scheduled for December 3 of 2012. It would take place at the Social Security Administration (SSA) Office of Disability Adjudication and Review in Madison, WI. I finally met my lawyer in person for the first time. He never had me prepared for what to expect during the hearing. They called us back into a room to review a CD with all the submitted files for my hearing. Only five to ten minutes to check the files before entering the hearing room in front of the Judge. Ten minutes? How is that enough time to review what we gave into evidence? Thankfully, the encrypted CD would be mine to keep.

Along with Judge presiding, a Vocational Expert would be present in the room. The Judge assigned the Vocational Expert, whether I can be competitive in the workforce. No Doctor was current or called upon to testify about my overall health.

During the hearing, there was no mention of my new diagnoses. The hearing went by so fast that the Judge never asked the Vocational Expert questions. Why didn't my lawyer mentioned I had two definite diagnoses that met the SSDI requirements? Never asked why as assumed I would find my new diagnosis files on the CD. When my hearing adjourned, I met up with my lawyer outside of the SSA Office. I asked him for his opinion on what my chances would be for approval of benefits. He replied 60/40. That was far from assuring.

After my hearing, I reviewed the CD files. To my surprise, all my APS and Lupus diagnosis files were not entered into evidence. I could not believe my eyes. Nothing. They had everything as I sent them all the emails to him and his staff. I called my lawyer to ask why he did not give my new diagnosis paperwork into evidence. He told me that his office never received any further information concerning my new diagnosis. He lied. For every email I sent his office personnel, I asked for a 'Received Receipt' and kept every copy. And thank God I did. I wanted to ensure my lawyer and staff had my new diagnosis, every piece of paperwork concerning my updated health records to plan accordingly. I was livid. When I talked to Tina, she suggested contacting a government official who works in Madison.

On a Monday, I contacted the local Office of Congresswoman Tammy Baldwin and explained my dilemma. How my lawyer lied to me, how I could prove it, how can I get this new information to the Judge? The woman I talked to was forthcoming, understood my situation, and asked me to email her everything I had, including my new diagnosis and any paperwork proving that my lawyer and his office did indeed receive my paperwork. I spent the rest of the day uploading all my paperwork, printouts of all my Emails, and anything else that would be relevant to my case. The following day, I received an Email from Congresswoman Tammy Baldwin's Office saying they sent my missing paperwork to the SSA Office. By the end of the week, I received two separate envelopes in the mail from the Social Security Administration. The first one was a copy of a letter addressed to "The Honorable Tammy Baldwin, House of Representative's office in Madison." The paperwork states that the information sent by her office was received and placed into my file. The Judge decided that upon more evidence, they found that a supplemental hearing was worthy and to have one scheduled. The second letter was sent to my lawyer, explaining new evidence was sent into the record by the Office of Congresswoman Tammy Baldwin. So much for my lawyer and staff saying that they never received my paperwork. I filed an official complaint with the State of Wisconsin Bar Association due to the law group's deception. The Bar Association gave notice to SCORS, informing my lawyer he will be barred from practicing SSDI cases in Wisconsin. And with that complaint, SCORS dropped me as a client, meaning I did not owe their law firm any money. Good. Now you see why a third-party law office suggested by an insurance company may sound logical when it is not.

Laurie and I were stressed out. I waited 14 months to get screwed over by a law office that did not have my best interests in mind. What more did we have to go through? Here we are in late December of 2012. I lost two jobs. I have been to many specialists in different cities in Wisconsin and now dropped from Long-Term Disability. I have not brought in any revenue for eight months, and money was tight. We turned the heat down in our house to 64–65 degrees throughout the day. I would be sitting at home with blankets and gloves on. Going to a restaurant like McDonald's with the kids was expensive. At least it provided the kids with fun, like playing in Playland. The only constant in our lives was camping in the Summertime. Camping is inexpensive. It gave us a chance to get away for a couple of days to take the kids swimming, have campfires, relax, and have fun. We wanted to make the most of our time together.

My lawsuit with the Disability Insurance company was at an impasse. I did not hear from anyone as no offers were made. Everything was pointing towards the court. Who knew how long that would take? We kept our fingers crossed and hoped for the best. Can we get any good news in life? I hit a point in life when I questioned my faith. I wondered if God did not want my family to have enjoyable lives, be happy, and have hope.

Come Summertime of 2013, I heard from my lawyer from Lincoln Hawk, S.C. The Disability Insurance company was ready to settle. We discussed what would be considered a fair offer. After talking to Laurie, we decided to accept the offer. The settlement would become official in September. As agreed within our contract, we owed the law firm one-third of our settlement. A small price to pay as we were living off one income for 2.5 years. One headache down, one more to go.

But another headache would appear. As we dealt with our future SSDI hearing, Laurie would end up hitting a deer on her way to work, totaling our van. Augh, why now? Welcome to Wisconsin, as deer are always on the move. Just look at the dead deer along our roads, and you will get the idea. "I believe" I spent my Sunday after Thanksgiving looking for a used van. It took a while, but eventually, we found one, our "white" van.

Finally, in January of 2014, my SSDI Hearing was scheduled to take place. I asked Tina from the APS Foundation to serve as an expert on both APS and Lupus, of which she was. My wife also attended and was asked some questions. Once again, a Vocational Expert was present to testify whether I could be employable and competitive in the workforce. This time around, a doctor was to testify via phone concerning my health. This doctor's background included Osteopathic Medicine, including Holistic Medicine. I was worried about her findings, diagnosis, and opinions concerning my health. Why was she needed as I already had an official APS and Lupus diagnosis? But the court needed a third party that had nothing at stake. Upon the doctor's testimony, she agreed that I met the SSDI guidelines twice. The Judge thanked her for her testimony. It did not take long, and the court was adjourned. Much like my prior hearing, the Judge did not need the Vocational Expert's testimony. On February 13, we received a letter in the mail that made our Valentine's Day weekend. The court found that the evidence in my case did indeed qualify for SSDI. Three long years of waiting. Winning my SSDI case made me feel like a Husband and Father once again. The feeling that I am supplying for my family once again. We will not be rich with me on Disability. At least it is something to live on.

It would only take a month before we received two years' worth of disability payments. As well, a monthly allowance was issued for me and my kids, arranged separately. My children will receive monthly payments until they turn 18 years old. We felt relieved and thought that just maybe, we can finally get on with our lives. We forgot what it was like to live everyday lives. On the horizon would be plenty of changes to come. And most of them would be far from satisfactory. The struggle for happiness would continue.

The APS and Lupus logo was designed by Desia Xiong. Desia Xiong is a Visual Communications student at Madison Area Technical College. She was commissioned for the purpose of designing the APS and Lupus logo and is expected to graduate spring of 2023.

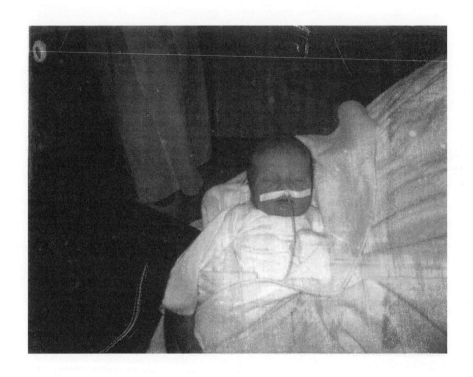

Only two days old and I am in the hospital for Volvulus surgery (Twisted bowel/intestine)

The Bo Jackson Sports and Fitness Center (The Bo). Nike Headquarters Global Business Academy, Beaverton, Oregon.

The Steve Prefontaine (Pre Hall) Building. Nike Headquarters Global Business Academy, Beaverton, Oregon.

October 16, 1999. Our Wedding day.

Our Honeymoon at the Sandals Royal Bahamian Resort (Nassau, Bahamas) October 1999.

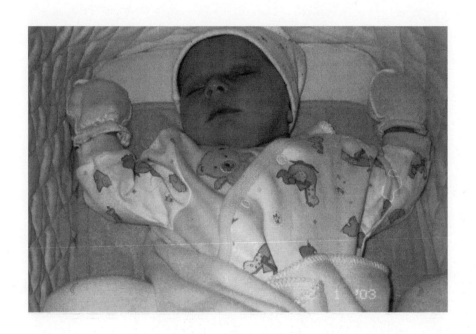

Our son, Sean Radke. January 2003.

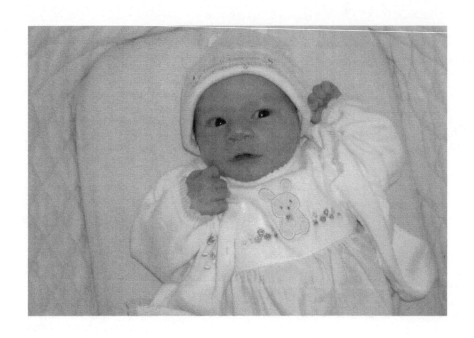

Our daughter, Alyssa Radke. June 2006.

Family photo for my Graduation Party. May 20th, 2007.

What would become normalcy in my life, napping with Thomas.

First (and only) big family vacation. Walt Disney World, Orlando, Florida 2014.

"Cabining" (Cabin rental + Camping).

Our Anniversary, October 16th, 2019

Proudly wearing my APS Foundation of America polo shirt.

Family photo 2020.

Me and Laurie (2020)

My 17th Birthday. Pictured with my Grandmother. I am wearing one of my favorite shirts. A bootleg Anthrax t-shirt with the words "I Am The Law" on the front and "Among The Living" in huge lettering on the back.

"The God of Thunder." KISS Reunion Tour, August 10th, 1996, Milwaukee, Wisconsin.

My weightlifting days paid off. I wish I still looked like this.

In loving memory of my parents.

Herbert Radke (11/26/1933 – 10/04/2018)
Joyce Radke (7/10/1936 – 10/10/2020)

SEVEN

One Step Forward, Two Steps Back

*"Keep your expectations low. This way you won't
be disappointed when things don't turn out."*
(Unknown)

Winning both disability cases was like winning the lottery. Imagine all the stress you have carried around throughout the years has disappeared. Life still had its difficulties, the "inescapable stress." However, knowing we would be soon receiving two-and-a-half years' worth of SSDI back pay certainly reduces your stress levels. It was like being reborn that you are alive again. Able to make plans to move forward with our lives (Please note – You are not going to get rich on monthly payments).

Both Laurie and I knew after the 2013 camping season we were outgrowing our current pop-up camper. The time was right to make a change. We needed a camper that offered more storage space, a broader floor plan, and bigger beds for the kids. By the end of January 2014, we started the search for a bigger camper. Not exactly the best time to search for campers just one month into Winter. It did not hurt to look and research websites like Craig's List. Sometimes you find things that are out of season. And with Craig's List, you knew everything would be close to the Madison area. By this time, we received the payment from our disability insurance lawsuit. Plus, we felt confident that we would win my SSDI case. As we budgeted, we knew how much we could afford.

By early February, Laurie found what seemed to be an ideal camper for us. The camper was only two years old, with plenty of space and well within our budget. Laurie called the owners to tour the camper as the owners had it fully popped up, allowing prospective buyers to walk through to view everything. Looking at the manual to view the floor plan was one thing. But having the camper up to view everything was ideal. The owners knew what they were doing. We found out that they lived in McFarland, less than thirty minutes away. As soon as Laurie hung up, we left for McFarland.

I will never forget that day. For starters, it was ice cold! In the middle of a polar vortex. The temperature with the windchill factor was 20-30 degrees below zero. As we walked inside the camper, both of us knew this camper was exactly what we wanted. The camper offered everything we wanted to move forward. We were there less than 15 minutes when Laurie wrote them a check. It was the right choice. The chances are good that if we waited, someone else would have bought it—no doubt in my mind. The owners were friendly enough to deliver the camper, late March. We could not wait to use our "new" camper. As a new vehicle, you think of all the cool things you look forward to doing. However, it is still February. Augh, the 2014 Camping Season, could not get here soon enough.

Once we received my SSDI back pay, we started making plans where we should allocate the money. Top priority, paying off any outstanding medical bills. Good riddance. Around the same time, we began making plans to take a family vacation. For over three years, we could not do much as a family beyond camping. And with everything we have been through, we wanted to get away to somewhere special. Somewhere Laurie nor I have been to before. A family vacation none of us would forget. And the likable choice was going to Walt Disney World in Orlando, Florida. Laurie would contact a travel agency to help us with all the hotel arrangements, flights, and transportation if needed. The rest we planned on our own. We thought going towards the end of October would be perfect. The kids would be off from school for two days due to Parent-Teacher conferences. Hopefully, the parks would not be as busy at this time of the year. The weather should still be warm by our standards. To this day, I can picture the kids' faces when we told them we were going to Walt Disney World! How big their smiles were! You could feel the excitement. Both me and Laurie we just as excited as this would be our first vacation since our Honeymoon. The only thing we did not do was get insurance if we needed to reschedule. Big mistake.

Things continued to remain busy round the Radke house. After nine years, we finally had the money to put in a deck/patio. We weighed our options, whether we wanted a deck or a patio. Building a deck would be too expensive. Maintenance would be an issue. I cannot do anything without someone's help. So, we explored all patio options available.

We talked with a couple of companies who had unique cement pouring options that would look great and would keep the price down, including the maintenance (Spraying on a lacquer every couple of years for protection from the weather). It would take us a couple of weeks before settling upon the company. This company offered stamped concrete, with various options in shapes and colors. It would only take a week to finish. Finally, we would have the opportunity to sit outside to relax, enjoy the weather, have fires, grill, and eat out as if we were camping. Patio furniture would not be an issue as we still had a table stored in our shed. It was collecting layers of dust and dirt for nine years. All the patio pieces were intact and remained in great shape. Perfect. No need to buy a new set.

We decided that this would be a great time to replace our sofa and loveseat. The couch was falling apart. You did not dare spin off one of the legs as chances were good that it would not go back in. They were 15 years old and survived moving three times. We bought the current ones when we were living in Oshkosh. Safe to say, we got our money's worth. We waited until massive sales/promotions would become available. We did not want to spend more than we had to. At that time, we were still finalizing our trip to Disney World.

Once the kids were back in school, we had all our contingency plans finalized for Disney World. For example, we would pick Epcot to spend the day. And with that, we needed to make reservations about the restaurants and special events we were interested in doing. Our package included three Fast-Track passes. The Passes allowed us to avoid using the long lines to move to the front quicker by using a different line.

October could not get here soon enough. We were counting down the days until we left for Disney World. Add our 15th Wedding Anniversary and Laurie's Birthday, and it felt like the time was right taking a family vacation. You could not help but have tunnel vision throughout this time. Life seemed to go in stride, without a care in the world.

But not everything would go as planned. What would be a common theme for us, every time we spent money on "luxury" items, things would break (One Step Forward, Two Steps Back). Items that were necessary to have. Starting in May, our lawnmower died. I only had it for a couple of years—what a piece of junk. The wheels were faulty and repeatedly came off. Bolts were stripped and impossible to turn. And challenging to replace, finding the exact sizes. We received no help from the store we bought the mower from. They give you it is "no longer under the store's warranty" or "You'll need to contact the manufacturer" story. They were playing the blame game. No offense, but we need a working lawnmower. It should last longer than two years. Forget about it. We will just deal with the wheels, including the use of duct tape. Maybe a month later, we had carburetor issues to the point the engine quit. Plus, the recoil snapped off. It would cost us $50 to fix. I ended up selling the mower to the person who fixed it for $50. Even draw. Off we go to get a new one. The store we purchased this lawn mower just lost a customer. Never again.

We were just weeks away from our vacation when our washer broke. It wobbled so badly, bouncing around at the bottom. It was funny to watch as it looked like the washer was ready to fly off. I called the company to have the washer fixed. The person who was working on the washer started it up and sat back to watch. He just shook his head. Soon after, he told us that fixing it would cost more than it is worth. It was nine years old. I have heard it plenty of times that new appliances usually last seven to ten years. They were right. We waited until we got home from Disney before shopping for a fresh pair.

Exactly six days before we left for vacation, I receive a frantic phone call from my Mother. They rushed my dad to the emergency room. She said that my dad shot back into his chair, clutching his lower side in pain. His abdominal aortic aneurysm ruptured. He has been living with one that did not require surgery, as it was never big enough for surgery. It was "only" 3mm big. The Cardiovascular Surgeons explained they do not perform operations until they are 5.5mm in size. (Remember this). All the information about my dad was all new to me. I picked my mom and drove to Madison. My dad needed emergency surgery on his heart. The Madison Hospitals where better equipped for his delicate surgery. Ironically, we would go to one of my least favorite hospitals. But it did not matter where we were. Time was of the essence. He had a rupture of his abdominal aortic aneurysm.

Once we got there and were about to perform surgery, the surgeon informed us that he had about a 10% chance to live. My brother would arrive about a half-hour after us. We had my sister on standby over the phone as she lives outside of Wisconsin. I do not recall how long he was in surgery, but it felt like an eternity. The surgeon who forewarned us about the 10% chance finally appeared. She found us and came over to talk. She said they were able to fix the valve, but he was far from safe. After surgery, Dad would be in Intensive Care, where he would stay for the next four weeks. Wires and gadgets were everywhere. The image reminded me of the back of my computer. As my family left, we knew that dad was in good hands.

It was late, "I believe" sometime between 10-11 pm, we all went home. My brother ended up driving my mom home. I swear I dozed off while driving home. I was tired and emotionally spent. It was a long night, and I was feeling the effects of my medication. I was equivalent to a drunk driver. I should have called Laurie to get me as I was not safe to be driving in hindsight. Nonetheless, I made it home in one piece.

What would prove to be the unpopular choice, we still went on vacation to Disney World. Without insurance, it was such a tough decision. My dad was touch and go. My mind was a mess. I never communicated with my family that if dad takes a turn for the worst, I will fly back. There was not much we could do. If we did not go, we would have lost a considerable amount of money.

Most importantly, I did not have the heart to look the kids in the eye and tell them that we will not be going to Disney World. I could not do it. What would they do at the hospital? They feared the place, much like a doctors' office. They know that nothing good ever happens at these places.

Finally, the day arrived, and we were off to Walt Disney World. I thought the kids would be scared to be on a plane for the first time. However, it did not even phase them. And they were sitting in the window seats. We ended up having the time of our lives! We were able to capture memories that I hope will stay with the kids for the rest of their lives. Maybe they can take their children and relive those memories. While we were there, with every passing day, my thoughts were still on dad. All I could do was hope for the best and prayed. Thankfully, I did not have to fly back home as he remained the same. Once we got back home to reality, it would not take long before bad things continued to happen. Payback from God for taking our trip.

I mentioned before, every time we spent money on "luxury" items, things would break (One Step Forward, Two Steps Back), "I believe" within a week of time home from vacation, early November, our microwave broke down. A burnt metal smell throughout the house. Phew! Open the windows, everyone! Much like the washer, it was the original microwave when we moved in. We got 9 years out of it. It was not long after shopping and buying a new washer and dryer, and we would be shopping and buying a new microwave. An early Christmas present.

It must have been a week or two (mid-November) after the microwave blew up when I would receive a distressing phone call from Laurie. She was on her way home from work when our "white" van's electronics stopped working: no headlights, turn signals, speedometer and dashboard lights, nothing. The only thing that was still working was the windshield wipers. Which were going at the fastest setting possible, and there was not a way to turn them off. Thank God it was early in the afternoon as it was light outside. Eventually, we took it to the vans brand dealership, got a loaner car, and waited to see what they find or hope to find. I told them to keep me posted.

After three to four days, the dealership called us to say they got the van's electronics working. Yet, when I arrived, there would be unwelcome news coming my way. They found corroded wires that led from the engine. Nothing else appeared broke or worn out. I nearly passed out when I saw the bill. It was almost $3,000, and that was no joke. Labor made up 80% of the bill. I asked them what they did that made the bill this expensive. The dealership told me they had to take out the front seats to get at the corroded wires. So much for keeping me in the loop. I would have told them you do not start until I spoke with Laurie. This way, we could weigh our options before moving forward.

Just before Christmas, my father came home. Seven weeks split between the hospital and hospice care facility—finally, some good news. Knowing my dad, he could not wait to sit in his recliner while watching television, mostly The Weather Channel or the Golf Network, and drinking a Whiskey Manhattan. An oxygen tank and mask were delivered to aid with his breathing. At times, he would have a difficult time catching his breath, primarily through his cough fits. Like he was hacking up a lung. Years of smoking taking their toll. Physically, he would never be the same. Regardless, we were all relieved he was finally home.

The 2016 Wisconsin Winter would be active in January. We were getting snow on what seemed to be on every fourth-day basis—dumping one to three inches of snow every time. We were lucky to avoid the big snowstorms, which would dump snow between five to eight inches. The amount of snow, and add windy conditions makes for one hell of a mess. It would be best if you had a snowblower during those storms unless you want to spend an endless number of hours shoveling. Welcome to Wisconsin, folks.

As luck would have it, my snowblower broke within a week of our son's Birthday. While I was snow blowing, I heard a bang, and the engine gradually stopped with smoke rising from the carburetor. After seven years, the engine died. It is time for a new one. Not having a snowblower was out of the question. A massive storm was coming our way. Meteorologists were predicting eight to ten inches of snow just days before his Birthday. Not a great time looking at buying snowblowers as they were scarce. We stopped at three places until we found one, we liked, especially since I would be using it. Luckily, we found an affordable one, manufactured by a company with an excellent reputation for making quality products. By the end of the day, I had a new snowblower in our garage. I had to wait and see if the snowstorm the meteorologists were predicting would come true. And they were right! We got eight to ten inches of snow, a foot. Time to fire up the new snowblower and see what it can do. I am proud to say this one kicked ass and got the driveway and sidewalks cleared.

In February, Laurie had trouble getting comfortable while lying down. She was experiencing severe pain throughout her chest area and could not sleep. Laurie tried sleeping on the couch and the lounge chair. Neither one helped. The pain was progressing with no end in sight. After two days with no improvement, she finally went to the doctor's office. Within 24 hours, two doctor appointments, and labs, we found ourselves at a Madison Hospital Emergency Room. Hmmm, sounds familiar.

It was a Saturday afternoon, and we had the kids with us. After running a couple of tests, they found Laurie had blood clots in both of her lungs!! As the doctor was reviewing Laurie's medical history, he mentioned the possibility of APS. I nearly fell out of my chair. He was talking about how APS is rare when I cut him off. I explained to him I had both APS and Lupus and was undoubtedly familiar with them. He felt Laurie's previous history of a miscarriage (9/11/01) and the combination of blood clots warranted testing for APS. It felt good that this Doctor was smart enough, open-minded, to consider APS. Luckily, those tests would prove to be negative.

I was on my phone for the better part of a half-hour while we were still in the emergency room. Our beloved daycare provider (Third set of Grandparents) and her husband came to the emergency room to pick up the children. They would take them to our house to pack enough clothes and other essentials as they would spend the next couple of days with them. Shortly after they left, Laurie would be admitted into the hospital and taken to a room. Laurie was out of it. She was sleeping on and off while nurses were working, setting up IVs, hooking her up to machines, you name it. Time seemed to fly once we got to her room. She continued to be in and out of sleep. I am not sure what time it was when I left. I thought it would be best to go home to get a good night's sleep. As Laurie was sleeping, I kissed her good night and left. What a long drive home. I was worried about Laurie. Thoughts of her dying scared me. The idea of being a single Father ran endlessly throughout my mind. What would the kids and I do without her?

As expected, I barely slept. It would not be long before I would find myself at the hospital. To my surprise, Laurie was awake. But she had a rough night. We both knew that it would take time to feel the medications' full effect kick in. I did not get too comfortable before the hospital staff asked about our health insurance. Laurie was in between jobs and had not reached her 90-day probationary period, meaning no health insurance coverage. We have plenty of paperwork to fill out, which required health insurance. While pale and in pain, Laurie would be on her phone to start the process of signing up for Cobra Insurance. COBRA (Consolidated Omnibus Budget Reconciliation Act) insurance helps provide coverage during that time. COBRA insurance provides coverage if you are between places of employment. The cost? $800 per month. And will end up needing two months' worth, a total of $1,600.

It was surreal by the manner they treated us. Did the entire hospital know we were uninsured? It sure seemed like it as getting a damn parking pass seemed impossible. The hospital required a library full of information, starting with our yearly income, any ongoing debts. Why do they need all of this? All I wanted was a parking pass, something that costs $12 a day. For God's sake, my wife is a patient. After thirty minutes of paperwork and seeing that I still had a way to go, I said screw it. I will pay the $12 instead of finishing the paperwork. I hoped she would not be in the hospital long. Laurie was making progress that Sunday but nowhere near ready to go home. She was having a difficult time breathing and required oxygen. The simplest of things, like getting out of bed, and she would be out of breath. It was extremely disappointing. "I believe" that no Doctors stopped in to see her. Everything fell upon the nursing staff. As if they have nothing better to do.

While talking with her two sisters, Laurie found out that her brothers had blood clots. She never knew as the subject never came up. What does the future behold for our children? Both of your parents have had clots. Your mom's side has a hereditary condition in their family, while dad's health issues were nonhereditary, as I was the only one on my side of the family with these problems. Yikes. It will be something they will have to pay attention to as they become adults. Something I thought about as I drove home for the night. I hoped Laurie would continue to make progress and have the possibility of coming home on Monday. That would be music to my ears. Once I got home, I called and gave updates to everyone. We will have to wait to see what Monday has in store for us.

Thank God my mom went with me on Monday. What a madhouse. There were six Doctors in the room in the morning, as they were using Laurie as a case study. But no updates. We would have to wait to ask if she still making progress. Would she be discharged today? Where was our medical six-pack of Doctors? We would not be seeing them anytime soon.

Shortly after lunch, the nurses had Laurie get out of bed and see how far she could walk. She was still on oxygen. Safe to say, she struggled walking. They would end up repeating the walking test a few hours later to a better outcome. Laurie was barely using any oxygen during her walk. A considerable improvement from the walk she took earlier in the afternoon.

The afternoon dragged on as if I were watching paint dry. The Doctoral six-pack made a brief appearance. Again, no news from the Doctors. The nurses were growing tired and frustrated with the Doctors. We sat there for hours waiting. I had to make new arrangements concerning the kids. Finally, around 7 pm, a Doctor stepped into her room and officially discharged her. We were thrilled, but Laurie looked so weak. She was still pale looking and was in constant pain. To this day, I find it hard to believe they discharged her. Was it because she had COBRA insurance? It took her the rest of the week before she felt normal. Her co-workers and friends were bringing over food while visiting with her. Awesome that she had people who genuinely cared. What a vast scare! She will be on blood thinners for the rest of her life.

Come April, Laurie calls me, and once again, the "white" van lost all electronics apart from the windshield wipers, precisely what happened in November. Gee, that was $3,000 well spent. We were lucky the first time this happened, as it was still light outside—unfortunately, not this time as it was close to sundown. Laurie was on the outskirts of Madison. I had to drive to Madison and had her follow me back home. All the while taking backroads to get home. Now, what do we do? There is no way I want to spend another $3,000. We had that van for less than two years, and it was sucking us dry. Time for a different van. We needed something with low miles from a manufacturer who has a reputation for quality vehicles that would last us for years to come. And we quickly found one—good riddance to the "white" van.

Without missing a beat, more problems would head our way. In April, our computer, three to four years old, died. You got to buy a new one as soon as possible as it controls everything in the house. In May, my PCP found that I damaged my L4 & L5 discs in my back. They would be affecting my sciatic nerve. The rest of your spine, down from the L5, is the S1 & S2 discs. And that is it, and you have reached rock bottom, meaning your butt. Not enough for surgery. Fine with me. I will learn to deal with whatever pain they may bring as I am not taking painkillers. I can feel floaty and euphoric without them.

Every year, we would go camping every Father's Day weekend. Camping that weekend has been a long-time tradition. It started so long ago that I do not even remember when it officially began. And like every year, this weekend would mark the start of our camping season. Usually, we plan on two to three trips per year, over Father's Day weekend, July 4th, and a weekend in late July or the first week of August. It would be a lot of work getting clothes and food packed. Once you got to the campground and had the camper all set up, it would be time to send the kids swimming while Laurie and I would kick back in our chairs to relax. Eventually, start a fire to enjoy the rest of the night.

As camping season was growing near, we needed to have a hitch placed on our newly purchased van. A new trailer hitch would prove problematic. When we bought the van, we assumed the van could pull the camper. As I researched the van's towing capacity and added the camper's weight, I knew it would be close to the maximum allowance of towing weight. That was worry some. I contacted a 'chained store' that place hitches regularly. I wanted to talk to the person who helped us the year before when we had a wiring issue. Thankfully, he still worked there. I explained my concerns whether the van would be able to tow the camper. He said he would check into things and call me back. It did not take long before he called back. He said with the right hitch, we "should" be fine. Great. I made an appointment to get a hitch put on, and like that, we would be ready.

Every year, we would always pack up and leave the Thursday before Father's Day. I would have both the van and the camper packed and ready to go as soon as Laurie got home. But we would have problems as I hooked the hitch to the camper. Our van sat lower than our "white" one. As I tried pulling out of our driveway, I stopped immediately. I could feel the entire back half of the van dragging along the concrete. It was a good thing I stopped and stepped out of the van to see what was happening. We were too heavy. I would have ripped the entire hitch off or do some severe damage to the van. Instead, I backed the camper towards the garage to see what I could do to fix this.

The obvious choice would be to unload the entire van and camper. Both had to be empty. I needed to see what would happen if I drove the camper around the block without any additional weight. The van and camper barely cleared as I pulled out of the driveway. I could tell how the van was having trouble keeping steady. We were dragging, with the front of the camper continuously hitting the van's bumper. And this is taking place while I was driving under 25mph. What is going to happen at 55mph? What is going to happen when we would pack our belongings back in? What will happen when all four of us are in the van?? Whether it was empty or not, the camper was too much for the van to pull. I made a poor choice listening to the installer. I trusted him. I explained what was happening and what we could do to fix this. We would need to add 'parts' to jack up the back end of the van. 'Parts' that would cost over a thousand dollars. Without them, we would be out of luck. It was our only choice if we wanted to pull the camper. He sounded like someone whose only concern was making a dollar. A fool and his money are soon parted. I should have trusted my initial instincts. I made a poor judgment in listening to him. So much for our weekend plans and the money we spent. You do not get refunds canceling on the same day as arrival.

Here we sit with a hitch on a van that cannot haul a beautiful camper that we loved. Something had to go, and that would be the camper. We never thought about our hauling needs before we bought another van. But we could not wait. The other van was unreliable. And we could ill afford to pour more money into a van with electronics issues. What about the wiring from the van's tailgate to the camper? What a mess. Hindsight is always 20/20.

It was not long after the debacle before we decided to sell the camper. It was heartbreaking to do so, but it was the right thing to do in retrospect. We posted the camper on a local seller's site to see if anyone would be interested. It took no longer than a couple of days before we sold our camper. We would sell it to the first couple to walk through it. A younger couple, with the woman pregnant. You could tell they were sizing up everything the same way Laurie and I did when we bought it. I moved the table out of the way to show that a crib would fit perfectly in that area. A few minutes later, they were ready to buy. Cool. We sold it for nearly the same price that we paid for it 17 months earlier. It was tough to see it go. At least we did not lose any money as it concerns the camper. That is good news. But we still had two more camping trips/reservations. And we were too late to cancel either one. What are we going to do?

We got the word out to everyone we knew who camped. Our friends we would be camping with let us borrow a tent to get us through camping weekends. The tent was what we needed for July 4th. We bought four foldable cots to sleep on as we did not want to lay on the ground. Laying on the ground was not an option! I am too old (and unhealthy) for that. The only issue for me was the weekend was hot. And I did not have anywhere to go, other than the campground's air-conditioned office and store. I would be tired from lunchtime on. It was around this time that I stopped going to the beach with everyone. I could not sit there exposed to the sun and heat. Let them have fun while I took a nap.

As the Summer moved along, little did I know that more heat-related challenges laid ahead for me. We live an hour away from Wisconsin Dells, The Waterpark Capital of the World. Every year, we would pick a day and go to one of the water parks. As the years passed, I quickly got cold after being in the water after thirty to forty-five minutes. I am talking shivering with goosebumps cold!! I started wearing compression clothing, consisting of a long sleeve shirt, and bicycling shorts that my swimsuit would go over to avoid this. I am sure I looked funny, but at least I was warm. My method was the only way I could prevent getting cold!! But this year, I noticed that more was happening beyond getting cold. I was drained, tired, and ready for a nap in less than two hours. What a weird sensation! I need to lay down in a shaded lounge chair. I am blazing hot from the neck up and ice-cold from the neck down! With my beach towel covering most of my body, I went to sleep. All the while, Laurie and the kids would be off having fun. Laurie would have to drive home as I was in no shape to drive. You cannot react as fast during driving when you are dead tired and beyond exhausted. Sadly, this would be my last time at a water park.

Our last camping adventure was a nightmare of epic proportions. And I am not trying to be sarcastic. We were trying a new campground that was horrible. Half the campground looked like an old trailer park, and the other half was the campground. The sites were terrible. We were on the side of a hill that had zero flat spots. That was our marked campsite. How are you supposed to pitch a tent and face downward with your cot? Nonetheless, we gave it a try. It was our last trip of the year, so let us enjoy it the best we could.

On our previous camping trip, July 4th, I placed a thick sheet of plastic underneath our tent to keep any type of moisture from coming through the bottom of the tent. Hey, this was not my first rodeo. I have spent enough time in a tent. Since we were on the hill, I used my tarps instead of the thick sheets of plastic. Unfortunately for me, it made the tent warmer. I wanted to block any moisture that could run down the hill. I wrapped the tarps along the bottom and part of the front side to protect the tent. Ideally, the tarps should push the water away to the sides of the tent. I was able to cover the tent sides with additional tarps. Set up the same way as the front side. Any water would be wicked away from the tent and continue moving downhill.

Other than the morning dew, we made it through the first night without any issues. I did not sleep the best. Our cots were far from comfortable. I should have taken photos of how we had the inside of the tent all laid out. We were creative and made efficient use of the space that was available. It turned out to be a great day. Mostly cloudy with temperatures in the upper 70 degrees. I was able to do things without feeling wiped out. I consider Summer days like that as a present. Enjoy those days if you can.

We were not so lucky on the second night. It started to rain after everyone went to bed. "I believe" it was roughly 2 am, awoken by rainwater flowing throughout our tent!! So much for all the work tying tarps to prevent water from getting in. Most of the things on the ground, including our duffle bags filled with clothes, were getting wet. We grabbed everything we could and hurried them into our van. What a mess. We were soaking wet from the rain. We tried sleeping while we were in our van. Once it was 8 am, we took the tent down and left one day earlier than planned. To this day, I can still picture the water flowing through the tent. The night's event would mark the last time we went tent camping. If we go camping the following year (2016), we will have to make changes. What type of changes? We had no idea. No more tent camping for us.

As you can see, getting that lump sum of money from SSDI gave us a false sense of security. We have asked ourselves plenty of times if we would not have spent a cent. Place all our money in the bank or buy stocks utilizing mutual funds. Would we have been able to avoid everything that happened? Probably not. But you get that taste of what it is like to enjoy life once again. Who could have foreseen what happened? It seems like you cannot avoid bad luck. I have heard it before that if you did not have bad luck, you would have no luck at all.

As I review this Chapter, I take stock of what has happened to us. On the bright side, we were able to buy a new camper, sofa/loveseat, patio, and a vacation to Walt Disney World. The bad includes lawn mower broke, the washer broke, my dad hospitalized for seven weeks, microwave broke, van repairs, snowblower broke, the van broke again/replaced with a different van, Laurie hospitalized, computer broke, damage to my L4 & L5 discs and to wrap it up, a hitch on our van that could not pull our camper that we eventually sold. All in nineteen months. Unbelievable. One step forward, two steps back.

EIGHT
Mentally Numb

"Do not confuse my bad days as a sign of weakness. Those
are actually the days I am fighting the hardest."
Author unknown

I can already tell that this chapter will be, figuratively, the death
of me. Or leave me mentally numb, as I named this chapter.
Emotionally, this has been a roller-coaster ride that never seems to
stop. And I am having a tough time thinking about what to write
in this opening paragraph. It has taken me months of thinking,
procrastinating, unable to plant my butt in my seat, in front of the
computer, and type.

In August 2015, because of my PCP's request, I returned to
Madison's earlier hospital/clinics to reestablish myself. The same
places I started within 2007. Here we go again. The good news was
I did not need a Hematologist as my PCP would manage that. The
only specialists I need to reestablish would be a Neurologist and
Rheumatologist. That sounded easy enough. Even though I miss
my Gundersen Doctors, I do not miss the traveling back and forth.

My first "Welcome Home" appointment was with a familiar
face. Neurologist #5 in Madison. She could not have been over
twenty-five years old. It was a routine exam. She wanted to know
the gap between 2012 until then. Explained about my experiences

here. As well, I added I traveled to Gundersen for second opinions and received what I felt was proper care. Impressive. I brought up neurologist #2, and the problems I experienced. Nicely, she said that he rubs people the wrong way. Unfortunately, this would be my only appointment with her. Last I heard, she left at the end of 2015. Oh great. Who will be my new Neurologist for my yearly checkup? I cringe at the thought.

Through a recommendation from my Cardiologist due to what happened to my dad's Heart valve scare, I had an appointment with a Cardiovascular Surgeon on 9/9/15. Two weeks prior, I had a Contrast Echocardiography test (CT 1 TAC with Contrast) performed. Simple procedure. The actual test lasts all of 10 minutes. Before the test, the nurse inserts an IV to administer the Contrast (made of either Iodine or Barium Sulfate). The Contrast administered takes place at the end of the scan. The Contrast makes your body warm for about a minute or two. It makes you sweat and gives you the sense that you peed your pants!!

I had Laurie attend my appointment with me. I was nervous and scared. To my amazement, the appointment with the Cardiovascular Surgeon was straight forward. He explained my aneurysm location with a heart model, explaining the procedure. Then we got on to the exciting part when we talked about the size of my aneurysm. Remember, the size had to be 5.5mm before he would do surgery. Mine was 'only' 4.2mm. I never asked why they would hold off surgery. The Surgeon explained no worries as they will watch me with a yearly visit, including the Contrast Echocardiography Test.

As a former manager, I always believed to be proactive instead of reactive. I am the type that wants to stay one step ahead of any issues or problems that may arise. And I would always have a backup plan if the first failed. But here I am, in a situation concerning the size of my aneurysm in my heart valve. I wondered why the Surgeon would wait until the 5.5mm size. 4.2mm is damn close to 5.5mm. Plus, the thought of what happened to my dad, how his aneurysm was not big enough to perform surgery. That is the type of reasoning that nearly killed him. To be honest, I would rather have the surgery as opposed to waiting. Let us be proactive, go in and get it fixed before there would be a problem (Reactive), as my dad. I do not want the same thing happening to me! The good news, over the years, my aneurysm has stayed the same size.

Otherwise, things remained uneventful. Something that was much appreciated. Our son was in 7th Grade and halfway done with his first of two years of Catechism for our church. Our daughter was in 4th Grade and was involved with dance classes/recitals. Our household, including Thomas, remained in good health. We still needed to find a solution if we were going to keep camping. I need air conditioning. And we do not have a vehicle to pull a camper. The only answer was to find campgrounds that have rentals. By the Summer of 2016, we started renting cabins to continue our camping family tradition. Renting cabins was our best choice. "Cabining" has become a staple in the family. More straightforward than having your camper. Less maintenance has a nice ring to it. Renting cabins may cost more, but they continue our Summertime fun. Our mini vacations if you will.

"Cabining" is a word I invented that combines cabins and camping. It is excellent renting cabins. Most are equipped with refrigerators and a microwave, giving us a chance to pack food and drinks accordingly. Rentals such as cabins, yurts, full-size campers, cottages, gazebos, and park models (tiny houses) are becoming more available. I am ready to buy a park model (tiny house). Downsizing sounds good right now. But if you are still using a pop-up camper, you have become the minority among campers. Most people have fifth wheels these days. They are huge! A house on wheels.

A trend I have seen over the years has been the lack of campsites for daily rentals for sites—those who only want to stay for a few days. Most campgrounds are 90%, if not higher, seasonal/permanent campers for year-round use. The campers are considered a second home, especially for "snowbirds." "Snowbirds" is a phrase given to retired people and live in the South from late Fall into early Spring. Then they live the dates in-between in their campers. Something I would not mind. Yet, it seems like a dream to live life like that.

Be able to take in the best that Mother Nature gives us. Escape the cold. They are most likely to be surrounded by warm weather. The simplicity. They are living the American Dream. Not stuck in a nursing home and going broke.

I have never seen how bad our health care system is when I compare it to working in nursing homes. Suppose you are a nurse, therapist, or in an administrative position. There are constant changes that take place. The corporation that owns the facility gets bought out by another company. Whether if it is the entire building or just one separate department, such as the Therapy Department. The new company comes in and makes sweeping changes. Precisely what happened to Laurie near the end of May in 2018. She found out that another company bought out the entire building (Nursing Home). The workers had two weeks to ready for the change. Two weeks? It would help if you started planning on changes, primarily health insurance—everyone's favorite subject. With Laurie's new health insurance, her deductible would increase to $7,000. That is a steep increase. Do not get sick.

My dad could not avoid the "Don't Get Sick" motto. His breathing was never the same after his triple 'A' in 2014. He needed a cane to help him get around. Oxygen machines. Air tubes. His constant hacking. Dad was never the same. Everything finally caught up to him in late September (2018). My mom called 911. The Rescue Squad took my dad to the emergency room. After a couple of hours, they would admit dad to St. Mary's Hospital in Madison. His breathing became so hallowed that death was imminent. He finally closed his eyes for good in the early morning of October 4th. I was the only one there. It was quick and hopefully painless. By the time I called my mom and sister, he was dead. We had his body cremated. His unburied ashes remained in a case. And will stay there until my mom dies. Whenever that time comes, both my dad and mom's last wishes were to be cremated. Together, the ashes would be forever committed to the ground, laid at their burial plot together.

By March 2019, we would end up moving my mom into a senior living apartment. We sold the house our family grew up. Words cannot explain how weird of a feeling to be walking throughout the empty house. Reliving all the good and bad memories. It was necessary to move mom as we did not want her alone in such a big house with different levels to get at essential items like the washer and dryer. They were in the basement. I do not want to envision my mom falling down the stairs into our basement. She needed to have everything on one level. Plus, there was nothing in our hometown. She settled in perfectly. We could not have asked for anything better.

Laurie would still endure more changes at work. Come September 2019, instead of the entire building, another company bought the therapy department. Great, more changes to come. Uncertainty flows throughout the therapy department. How will this affect her job? How about health insurance? It seems like every year there are changes, and those changes are certainly not for the better. $225 per paycheck (every two weeks) goes towards health insurance. Her health insurance plan has deductibles reaching as high as $13,000. Let that sink in. $450 a month to pay for insurance with deductibles that will bankrupt you. How could anyone afford that? I said it before, and I will say it again, do not get sick.

From a manager's viewpoint, this is precisely what the company wants is to save money. Get rid of the current staff and bring in those fresh out of college. Most who went to college would be happy to find a job in their chosen field shortly after graduation. And the chances are good that you are in debt. A job that pays is an essential choice to make. No matter how much the job pays, you do it because it does pay. Money pays the bills.

Eventually, the subject of health insurance rears its ugly head. Can you afford to spend $450 a month? How about the $13,000 deductible? That is a significant risk. Suppose something serious happened to you. You reached your deductible. You would have $6,000 total deducted from your paycheck just to have insurance for the entire year. Now you have paid out $13,000, reaching your deductible. In one year, you could spend $19,000 on healthcare. Once again, do not get sick.

Laurie's employers and their continuous changes and lack of security have held our family back from taking any vacations. You do not need to be spending unnecessary money on luxury items. And you need to hope and pray that things do not break down. In 2017, we were planning to take a vacation to Tennessee for a week. We would be driving to save money. We had the place all picked out. We had plans which day, where we would visit. We knew our daily budget. But significant changes are heading to Laurie and the entire therapy department. Sorry kids, but we cannot go anywhere this year. Next year. We did not bother "thinking" about a vacation in 2018. It proved to be a wise decision. Another company bought the entire nursing home—too much uncertainty to be spending money.

Once again, in 2019, job changes affect more vacation plans. We had a vacation planned in August to spend four nights away to Door County (Wisconsin). An area is known for its tourism. Both me and Laurie have been there three times, twice at a Bed & Breakfast (pre-children) and camping (with children). We looked forward to getting away. We had a suite rented with three bedrooms, a kitchen, and a patio to view the lake. We wanted to do something rememberable as Sean was going to be a Junior in High School. And time is ticking if we are going to take a vacation before he graduates high school. Going back to Disney World would be awesome. Yet, a yearly theme, recent changes were coming in the form of the therapy department was sold.

It is bad enough having the department bought out from under you. But there would be sweeping changes to the therapy department. As modifications to "therapy reductions and reimbursement shifts amid the transition to the Patient Driven Payment Model (PDPM) on October 1st of 2019, but concerns may soon shift to another looming therapy change—this time under Medicare Part B."

As published in Skilled Nursing News, writer Lyndee Yamshon (11/17/19) states that "The Centers for Medicare and Medicaid Services (CMS) has proposed an 8% cut in physical therapy rates in the final Physician Fee Schedule (PFS) for calendar (year) 2020." She continues that "Medicare Part B patients make up 70% of the average nursing homes resident population, some of whom receive therapy. These particular patients are long-stay individuals who typically remain in the care of nursing homes and in need of constant around-the-clock attention-until they most likely die." The power of positive thinking.

The article continues, "While a Medicare A patient might get rehab in a nursing home because they broke a hip, Medicare B patients stay longer than one hundred# days and are not under the PDPM (Patient Driven Payment Model) model. For long-stay residents, Medicaid covers the nursing home stay, with ancillary services such as doctor visits and rehab therapy billed through Medicare Part B. These patients are known as dual residents, or patients with both Medicaid and Medicare B coverage. At the same time as the 8% therapy cut, the rule increases payments to doctors who see Medicare patients in their offices under fourteen codes for office and outpatient visits—a classification known as "E&M," or Evaluation and Management."

"As with PDPM (Patient Driven Payment Model), CMS (Centers for Medicare and Medicaid Services) considers the physician fee schedule to be budget-neutral—so when CMS increases one category of payment, they must decrease other codes to neutralize the spike. In this case, CMS made the E&M slice bigger than 40%, with therapy among multiple specialty services suffering pay cuts to offset the gains. Therapy is one of the victims to offset those increases. The patients cannot take this cut. There's no reason rehab therapy for these frail patients should sustain a cut."

According to Katie Engelhart for NBCNEWS.com (11/29/19), "Advocates, experts, and the federal government say that nursing homes tend to evict low-income, longer-term residents who receive Medicaid, to make room for shorter-term rehabilitation patients who are covered by Medicare. Medicare reimburses nursing homes at a higher rate than Medicaid, so it is more lucrative for facilities to house Medicare patients who stay for short stints before recovering and moving elsewhere. In California, for example, the average state Medicaid reimbursement for a nursing home is $219 per day, according to the California Association of Health Facilities, while Medicare may reimburse more than $1,000 per day, but only for up to 20 days, when patients must begin paying part of the fees. Medicare coverage ends completely after one hundred days."

In her article, she quotes Deborah Pacyna (Director of Public Affairs at the California Association of Health Facilities, who says "that California's Medicaid program, Medical, does not provide adequate funding to care for many patients with complicated health issues and behavioral disorders. Medicare pays more. Those people are rehab patients; they are in and out. That is how they (Nursing Homes) break even. Society's problems are manifesting themselves on the doorsteps of nursing homes. Nursing homes are legally allowed to evict residents under several conditions: if a resident's health improves sufficiently; if his presence in the facility puts others in danger; if the resident's needs cannot be met by the facility; if he stops paying and has not applied for Medicare or Medicaid; or if the facility closes. Facilities are bound under federal law to give 30 days' notice, in writing, and to work with the resident on a transition plan. While some residents are issued formal discharge letters with advance notice, others are asked or pressured to leave with 'no due process rights, no notice.'"

"But the federal government has made changes that reduce fines against nursing homes that harm or endanger residents. Nursing homes used to receive fines for each day a violation was seen, but after a change the Trump administration implemented in July 2017, nursing homes are now usually fined just once per retroactive violation. Meaning a nursing home that evicts a patient and refuses to admit the person may be fined one time, instead of every day that the resident is denied a bed."

What you read may seem like simple changes and a way for companies to remain profitable. Every business needs to survive in our country. But those changes have come with dire consequences. Since then, my household has not been the same. It does not satisfy our government as they now want to go after me, the disabled.

A post on December 12th of 2019, written by Alfred Lubrano, titled "Trump administration proposes Social Security rule changes that could cut off thousands of disability recipients." Mr. Lubrano reports, "The Trump administration is proposing changes to Social Security that could end disability payments to hundreds of thousands of Americans, particularly older people and children. The new rule would change aspects of disability reviews—the methods by which the Social Security Administration decides whether a person continues to qualify for benefits. Few recipients are aware of the proposal, which is open for public comment through January."

Our politicians seem to be on a crusade to make any, if not all, changes to programs considered entitlements. Social Security is the most significant entitlement. It is said that Social Security is running out of money. They should privatize money before it is too late. Alfred Lubrano further explains, "Critics of the plan liken it to the administration's efforts to cut food stamps, among other entitlement programs, with insufficient information offered to explain curtailing benefits."

He continues, "Those already receiving disability benefits are subject to so-called continuing disability reviews, which determine whether they are still deserving of compensation for an injury, illness, or other incapacitating problem as their lives progress. Not everyone gets reviewed within the same period. A person with a grave illness such as Lou Gehrig's disease (ALS) in a category called 'Medical Improvement Not Expected' and needs review every five to seven years." Nice of our government to label ALS 'Medical Improvement Not Expected'. The chances are good that the patient will be dead and will no longer need benefits.

"Medical Improvement Not Expected" is one category proposed. The other two, 'Medical Improvement Expected' and 'Medical Improvement Possible.' According to the post, "All three categories are based on existing medical standards meant to help officials decide whether the benefits remain warranted. The proposed rule change 'Medical Improvement Likely,' which would mandate disability reviews every two years, creating an added 2.6 million reviews over the first 10-year period. This category makes little sense. Medical conditions deteriorate as already unhealthy people of age, and no evidence exists that such beneficiaries are 'likely' to improve. Labeling them that way is a 'radical departure from past practice as there's no medical or scientific basis to say they'll get better."

Writings by Mark Warshawsky (current Deputy Commissioner for Retirement and Disability policy) at the Social Security Administration, who has proposed eliminating the criteria of older age, low education, and unskilled work experience in determining eligibility for SSI (Supplemental Security Income) and SSDI (Social Security Disability Insurance). In March, the conservative Heritage Foundation, which often supplies underlying rationale for Trump administration policies, released a statement that said, 'Factors of age, education, and experience do not and cannot cause workers to be disabled from performing all work…only physical and mental conditions…should qualify individuals to receive disability insurance benefits."

None of this makes a whole lot of sense. Especially the category labeled 'Medical Improvement Possible.' I have been trying to research this category and have produced nothing. Just having the word 'Possible' concerns me. It is very suggestive. Is it possible, depending upon the person or its usage? I find this troublesome. Will they label those with chronic health issues that they could work?? That is a scary thought!! I do not need uncertainty when it comes to disability changes: stress and tension.

The year 2020 will undoubtedly be the year of upheaval. Before those changes took place, Laurie was already working one full-time job and two part-time jobs in therapy. Both part-time jobs are considered PRN, or as needed. No guarantees if the company will need you. Throughout the years, a length of time that I do not recall she has been working every Saturday. Laurie feels that she better take on any added hours to avoid money issues due to hours' inconsistency. We have always been in restraint due to my disability as it affects our income. Yet, another life-altering change you could think of has occurred in the Radke household.

Now her full-time job has been reduced (I call it a demotion) to a PRN status. Meaning no health insurance. Laurie felt this was the company's plan as soon as they bought the therapy department. And shortly after the Holidays, the change became official. On a Friday, January 3rd, mid-afternoon, the company called her to tell her the news. They wanted to wait until after the Holidays.

Since January, Laurie has been looking for a new job. There was nothing available for full-time PTA's. At the facilities she currently worked at, the only available jobs were in nursing. Nursing positions are always open. Companies barely need physical therapy workers. The industry was continually changing and not for the better. People she used to work with left the medical field. They were tired of the constant pressures. It reminds me of teachers within our school district and surrounding areas who left teaching entirely. The input I have received is they are tired of all the changes. It was stressful, and they grew tired of an industry they used to love and were passionate about. Yet, it was always constant pressure to do more with less. It is not worth it anymore. That is what Laurie needs. A clean break from healthcare. There would be good news as she was hired in August for a Physical Therapist Assistant position.

In February, I ended up in the emergency room. As I helped my neighbor snow blowing, I lost my footing on the ice and fell on my back. Luckily, I did not hit my head. Bad news, I sliced my tongue with my teeth and needed a couple of stitches to stop the bleeding. No good deed goes unpunished. Now Laurie's crown fell off one of her teeth. We scrambled to call dentist offices to get the crown re-cemented. Upon her appointment, the Dentist informed Laurie that the current crown could not be re-cemented due to the tooth's size. Only a new crown would work. They also found the tooth next to the current issue needs work as well. Is not that great! We know where our tax refund money will go towards paying.

The Covid-19 Pandemic hits. People lost jobs or furloughed. Stay at homeschooling via virtual classes instead of in-school courses due to the shutdown. People were buying products in mass quantities, especially toilet paper, soap, and hand sanitizer. All Winter and

Spring sports were canceled. The University of Wisconsin Women's Hockey Team was poised for another run to repeat as National Champions. The Milwaukee Bucks were the top team in the NBA. Add this to the list of 2020's disappointments. The list keeps growing.

In mid-March, most schools closed due to the Pandemic. School Districts had two weeks to design a game plan on how to teach classes over the Internet. Parents had to make difficult choices whether they could leave their children at home. Could they go to their daycare providers? What about the Covid-19 risk? Should you have "outsiders" in your homes? March began the "What If'" questions that still exist today. As I write this, the new 2020-2021 school year will be starting Virtually. It is unknown whether this will be one quarter, half the year, or the entire year. What if the Pandemic becomes worse during the late Fall into Winter when the regular flu season hits? What if a statewide/nationwide shutdown is needed to stop this Pandemic? The uncertainty is stressful. I had a feeling the next school year, which started in September, would be virtual. It was. Not the way I would like my son's Senior Year to start. He has already missed the opportunity of Junior Prom. And Homecoming. Better to side on the err of caution.

During this time, my daughter's confirmation would be delayed indefinitely due to the Pandemic. Nothing could be done. Due to living in a small town, our church is not that big. Church services were not held inside due to Covid. Only outside in the parking lot. October was a possibility. That is a long wait. Our church did not choose but to extend the confirmations back, hoping that the Pandemic would be gone, and life would return to normal.

My mom is a two-time breast cancer survivor. She has also battled skin cancer, keeping it at bay with medication. She stopped taking the medication as the side effects were rough. A routine appointment in April would reveal that her cancer was increasingly spreading throughout her body. She was having trouble with her breathing. Walking down the hallway would require her to take breaks for her to catch her breath. We knew she was slowly dying. My mom did not want to know what was happening. She has said multiple times that she is ready to go home, meaning Heaven. We started making plans to move my mom to my sister's house. She has more room, large open areas for my mom to access quickly. My sister is a Women's Health Nurse Practitioner and would know all the plus and minuses my mom would go through. All of us agreed to the date when we would move her in late June. Another 2020 challenge.

I had a dentist appointment scheduled in April for routine cleaning. Since the spread of Covid-19 was making its way across Wisconsin, mandatory precautions were in place. Nobody could sit in the waiting area. When a patient arrived, they had to call the front desk to let them know they were there. And according to their guidelines, a patient would have to wait for a staff member to come to get them—this would-be common practice amongst dental and orthodontist facilities. No big deal, as it was the sign of the times.

My appointment did not go as planned. I went through the precautions in place and waited for one of the dental personnel to get me. I waited ten minutes before someone comes out. However, they no longer accepted my insurance. I asked when the insurance change became effective? They said the beginning of the month. I wondered why no one contacted me about this change. It was too late to contact me. Too late? They called me weeks earlier to confirm my information, including my insurance. I had no choice but to turn around and go home and contact my insurance. I found a new dentist but had to wait until September to get an appointment. Ten months between my last appointment.

Laurie saw Covid-19 makes its way into the nursing homes. A few patients tested positive. Before you know it, everyone from patients to workers required testing. Laurie knew she would test positive as she suddenly lost the taste of food. And tested positive. Thank God the symptoms only lasted a few days. But her diagnosis meant our entire household would need to be quarantined for fourteen days. Since we rarely go anywhere of importance, quarantined was not a big deal. The only event that took place was our great nephew's first birthday. Unfortunately, we had to cancel as the date landed within those fourteen days. We did not want to miss the party. But there was nothing we could do.

Before you knew it, June was fast approaching, meaning my mom would be moving. That was weighing on the back of my mind. Yet, June would throw another curveball at us as Thomas was sick. He stopped eating and was lethargic. His organs were shutting down. What could more happen this year? It was painful to decide to euthanize him. More distressing to watch it. But I wanted to be there for his last breaths. I wanted him to see me staring eye to eye before he dies. I hope he is at peace. I miss him. See you at The Rainbow Bridge.

The fateful day of June 28th, better known as Mom's Moving Day, finally arrived. We could not have asked for better weather. Sunny with a temperature around 80 degrees. My sister and brother-in-law were able to use a friend's truck and trailer to haul most of Mom's items considered necessities. Those left behind would end up split amongst everyone or donated. Either way, we needed to have mom's apartment emptied by the end of August.

It was not more than a month before my mom's health decline accelerated. My brother, sister, and I would have Sunday conversations concerning mom. Talk about the changes mom was going through. Any updates from her social worker and nurse. My sister would send a text if something minor happened. Things did not take long that a Sunday only conversation was not enough. Soon it would be twice a week. By mid-August, mom's health was significantly changing. I thought it would be essential to spend time with Mom before things worsen.

I flew down to spend quality time with my mom. She was watching TV, playing the card game cribbage, anything to keep her mind at ease. I was available to spoil my nephews whenever I could. My brother joined us three days after me. He felt the same way I did. Having a chance to spend time with mom as this would be our last time together. I knew there is no way I could fly down again. Thanks to group calls with my siblings, my sister informed us of mom's changes. Keeping me informed brought peace—strange thing to say. However, I knew she was in good hands with my sister.

Then the last couple of days finally arrived. My sister called, saying mom is down for a day or two. Simply put, her entire body was shutting down. Part of me wanted to be there. Yet, most of me did not. I want to remember her the way she was before I left. It was around 4:30 pm on October 10th when my sister called, giving me the bad news. She died peacefully to the song "Amazing Grace."

We buried my parents' ashes on October 18th. Tricky things to do were holding onto straps as you lower them into the Earth, saying my final goodbye to my parents. I love both of my parents. But I had a special bond with my mom. As I wrote before, she was my rock during my quest for answers to my health. She was always there for me. Some might say that is what moms are there for.

What an ugly year. But the bad news kept coming. On Tuesday, December 8th, my wife received a stuffed envelope from the Social Security Administration office. My Disability case is under review. They wanted fifteen pages worth of material, testimony, if you will, to list all the Doctors I have seen over the last twelve months. My deadline was January 2nd, 2021. A tight window.

I sent the requested paperwork concerning all twelve months of Doctor notes, via USPS Registered Mail. Better not lose my papers! Officially fifty-one pages. You name it, and it was there as I mailed the packet back. I cannot help but wonder, will my paperwork be used as evidence? I believe my case has been predetermined, found non-favorable, meaning I can work. Or, as the vocation expert would say, "I'm able to be competitive in the job market." To date, I have not heard a word.

I cannot think of anything crueler. First, to question my Disability. I was not getting rich on our monthly payments. Secondly, to do this during a World Pandemic. Third, there are over 800,000 people unemployed. And if I lose my benefits, what would I specifically write for being "off" and "out of work" for ten years? I was in a car accident that took me ten years to recover. I would need to show my illnesses as I would lose coverage under the American Disabilities

Act. How will I find a full-time job with benefits to cover my medications? I could find myself back at square one. I am mentally numb. Things were not easy to get on disability. And now it seems that I will need to fight to stay that way. I can only hope that my evidence given will be enough to keep me on disability.

Come April, the State of Wisconsin SSA, mailed new paperwork, asking essay questions with a tighter return date. My poor wife spent over two hours filling out the paperwork. Needing to go into specific details and updates, of which there is not. I truly do not understand. The stress, from the paperwork to waiting for their decision. It is depressing and my anxiety levels are higher than they should be. I am paranoid. Is someone watching me? The paperwork they need makes you want to quit. But I am a fighter. I will go down swinging.

NINE

Changes and Challenges

"Fear kills dreams. Fear kills hope. Fear puts people in the hospital. Fear can age you. Fear, ladies, and gentlemen can hold you back from doing something that you know within yourself that you are capable of doing. But it will paralyze you. What is the benefit of allowing fear to hold you back of not stepping out on life and taking life on? What is the benefit of that?"
(Author unknown)

I keep the following quote to heart as I fell in love with the context, courtesy of the bodybuilding website Kulturistika.com. It refers to how people struggle with their thoughts and mind. I love it and relate to it. With that, I would like to share it.

"The bible says it is with the mind that we serve the Lord. It is with the mind that we serve the Lord. The mind is the battleground. It is the place where the greatest conflict is. There are more people in this room having trouble in their mind than there are people having trouble with their finances. The struggle is in your mind. This is why we have people who go to bed tired and wake up tired. Slept eight hours, and you woke up still tired. The reason you woke up tired is that you got sleep but you did not get rest. Your mind has been in turmoil all night long. You have been wrestling in your sleep. Have you ever woken up and your bed was wet? The bed is all tore up, just like you have been into a fight because your mind has not rested. Your body went to sleep, but your mind is still caught up in a warfare. Your mind is the battleground. Pick somebody and tell them the enemy is after your mind. Out to worry you to death, out to stress you to death, out to break you down. Out to make you quit, out to make you think that you cannot get up. Out to make you give up on your dreams. The warfare is in your mind. It is not on your checkbook. It is not on your savings account. It is not on your job. The fight you got to fight is your mind."

At the end of Chapter Eight, I cannot start with this Chapter by making jokes or using sarcasm. It just cannot happen as this Chapter is essential. It is tough to talk about the progressive changes the diseases continue to wear on your body. Our bodies are unique. It should come as no surprise that our bodies react differently to our abnormalities. Some for the better, some for the worst. The same line of thinking when adding medications to the mix.

The physical changes might be simplistic and reactionary to your environment. You are exposed to many and unique challenges that most will never understand. By now, I am sure most are becoming aware of the physical changes. Sore joints. Headaches. Blurred vision. Low energy. Pain/discomfort in areas that you never dealt with before. And I am just scratching the surface with the physical changes.

Start with chronic fatigue. I know what you, the reader, are thinking that "Chronic fatigue is not a physical change." True. But it slows you down from what you want to do. There is no pain involved. But when the fatigue hits, it hits like a ton of bricks. Fast and furious. You ask yourself, "What the hell happened to me?" You can drink all the coffee your kidneys and bladder can hold. But it usually does not help. Please give me my couch, both the TV and our soundbar remotes, my water bottle, and lay down. That is all you can do.

Before bad weather arrives, my body goes into a pounding headache and fatigue funk. Sinus pressure. Joint pain. When the Barometric (or Atmospheric) Pressure changes, your body reacts accordingly. The lower the pressure, the higher the pain. Joint pain can be at its worst as your muscle fibers expand.

It is the dizzy spells that cause a lot of problems. Enough to where I do not drive if the severity of it hits before I leave the house. No matter if I am driving or just a passenger. Nausea usually kicks in. Some only last one minute. Others up to five minutes. I have had one recently that was ten minutes. No kidding. I sent an email to my Neurologist asking if it was time to schedule an appointment, as it was planned on a two-year basis. The ten-minute dizzy spell was scary and eye-opening. What would have happened if I were driving?

My knees hurt so bad that walking up and down the step in my house seems like a challenge. Mind you, I am in no need of a chair lift. I can make it, but you can feel the fatigue that sets in. It could be physical, burning some of the strength you need to get around. It could be mental, the fatigue due to the lack of energy that it took to walk up and down the steps. Like your body needs a timeout. Much like playing hockey. After a couple of minutes of ice time, you in need of a break, a line change if you know and understand the game. Time to sit down, replenish the fluids you lost by sweating, and giving your body rest until you are called upon to play after a couple of line changes. Hockey and its line changing analogy is a perfect way to explain what I sometimes experience walking up and down the steps.

The inactivity is a bear to deal with. For over half my life, I have been active, working out. It became an addictive lifestyle. Working out was my ideal way of dealing with the bad things going on with my life. It has always been there. APS and Lupus changed that. Thanks to them, I have put on weight. Inactivity and medications have helped in my weight gain. The lack of interest is important. You have plenty of distractions, like binge-watching television, checking Facebook. I know it happens to everybody. But if your body feels good and your energetic, do not sit. Try to do something, even if it is something simple like vacuuming for 30 minutes. At least you can be proud of yourself for doing the work. Just do not fall into the Binge TV trap.

Whoever coined the phrase "Binge Watching" was right on the money. With all the various apps, you can spend a whole day watching a specific show. Watch an entire season in a matter of days. No more experiencing "The Infamous Cliffhanger" when you must wait a week to find out what happens next. Not anymore. Binge-watching is equivalent to a cookie. You eat a cookie, and you are at once satisfied. But you start to think, "Hey, one more isn't going to kill me." Before you know it, you have unknowingly eaten six cookies. You are binging!! And binging on TV shows will lead to binging on food unless you have extraordinary willpower.

Trying to find the most effective help to relieve conditions can take a long time. Certain medications may not be as useful as other medications. You see yourself bouncing from one to another. Collaborating with your Doctors and your insurance company to help keep the cost down. That can be another struggle. You may find adding over the counter remedies can have an impact on your body. Usually nothing good. I decided to increase my Vitamin D3. It came as a recommendation from a Dietitian. Using them sent my INR crazy high. Waste of money. It is a challenging task when you need to get your INR checked when you are fresh off switching medications. It is easy to forget, but you need to ask yourself, what are my current prescription or medication's side effects?

Are the side effects short term or could they be long term, causing damage to vital organs? Will the cost or side effects outweigh the benefits? Just reading the warnings and the possible side effects a prescription drug poses can be overwhelming. Is this worth taking? Could it make things worse? What about taking an anti-depressant that has side effects such as may cause suicidal thoughts?? Why would you take a drug that supposed to help depression only to have the possible side effect as may cause suicidal thoughts? I cannot help but wonder if I am taking a medicine to help with the side effects caused by another medication I am taking? And what is the potential for future damage to organs such as my heart, liver, and kidneys?

You cannot help to be curious what years of taking one medication are doing to the body. I have been on acid reflux medication for over twenty years. The long-term use of acid reflux medication may cause bone loss. Whether it is right or proven by the FDA, I am not 100% certain as I read it within a bodybuilder's magazine from England. But it makes me wonder if that is true. If I have suffered bone loss? My problem is that I have never had it checked out by a Doctor. I cannot tell you why other than monetary issues.

What about taking a generic drug? Do they work like the brand name medication? If so, would there be any changes to your body? Some patients cannot switch to a generic drug, as it is not as effective as the brand name. Sometimes, the drug's side effects are worse than the brand name, or the brand name has no side effects. The insurance company may reject the medication as the brand name drug is too expensive. It is part of a tiered plan. It happened to me taking medication for high cholesterol. One was working fine for a couple of years. An insurance change takes place, and they will not pay for this medication. You must settle for the next medication allowed within the tiered system. You are settling for what could be a less effective drug that costs the same as your prior drug.

The costs of medications are a nightmare to deal with. According to a Bloomberg report (7/16/18), average prices for Rheumatoid Arthritis and other autoimmune medications increased by 40% over three years (2015-2018). Ouch! Remember those figures. What are the odds those prices will decrease? I doubt it.

Medications, or drugs, can be a nightmare of epic apportions. Big Pharma has you paying top dollar for medicines that cost pennies on the dollar to make. The company and its shareholders get to live a comfortable life while you can barely afford your medication or pay your bills, depriving you of your own American Dream. If you watch any TV during the late morning or the evening news, commercials are full of medication ads. It is incredible, as there is a medicine for every ailment out there. Or scare you into believing what you may have, placing thoughts inside your head, knowing that you should take this medicine. It may help me. We have become so programmed into thinking like this that Americans take 70% of the world's medications. Is there something other countries know we do not? Are their ways simplistic? Affordable? Have they found a better way to do things that are more effective than just using drugs?

I have been in a situation when I started siphoning expensive medication. What choice do you have when you cannot afford your medication?? It never crossed my mind about the potential dangers I could be putting myself in. What could happen to those around me? Will it affect my driving? If so, am I placing others in trouble, passengers, and other drivers alike? How about all the medications I take daily? Will they be just as effective as usual? I know what I was doing was wrong and dangerous choices. I got lucky as nothing happened. Hopefully, I never have to make that choice ever again.

It is hard to escape the insecurity from daily living. To enjoy life when you are feeling awful. I have come to the point that this is how life is going to be whether I like it or not. Dwelling upon your issues is like grieving your former self, your former lifestyle. So, I better stay strong as others are depending on me. And I hate being a quitter, something I was during my youth. I want to be known as being healthy—someone who can stand up to adversity. Be able to accept, what is done is done. Do not play the victim. Do not dwell upon it as you cannot change things. So, stop living in the past and live for today. Well… it is not that simple.

I cannot help but wonder if others receive the necessary support from within their own family. Impossible to have that question truthfully answered, but I did research it. Forty-five percent received tremendous support from everyone around them, including family & friends. Fifteen percent said that their support was fair, from their husband/wife/life partner, children, parents, in-laws, or siblings. The most negative number I came across was 40% receive no support at all. I heard everything from a lack of understanding to being attention seekers. I find those numbers astonishing!! Fifty-five percent receive mediocre to no support. I spoke before about those close to you who will give you the least support. It is upsetting, disturbing, and cruel.

But the numbers do not lie. It is not like we are going out of our way to seek attention. So, what gives?

There happen to be feelings that really can do a lot of damage if not dealt with properly. Depression and Anxiety are brutal and are a nasty one-two punch to have and manage. How does one feel good about yourself when you feel useless, isolated from society, ostracized, if you will? It is not easy to put into words when you tell people how you feel. More time than not, they tell you that you should not feel that way. Yet, I do feel that way. I find it tough to see how my life has any meaning outside of our house, beyond my family. I tried volunteer work but was finding myself in the same situation as working a job. My feeling of being alone is horrible, torture to the human soul. There is a lot of scary things in this world, but none worse than loneliness. I am married with two children and a cat, and I feel alone. It is easy to feel alone in this world.

Stress is another silent health issue that has a drastic impact on the body. It gets talked about yet hard to control. The pressure is an everyday event. No one needs it, yet we let it bother us. The New York Times printed an article by Dr. Huan Song from the University of Iceland on 7/12/18, saying, "Stress really affects long term health. It affects not only psychiatric health but leaves people vulnerable to other diseases. There are many treatments now available for stress-related disorders and it's important for people to get treatment early." Another quote includes, "Stress is known to cause physiological changes, including immune function but evidence that links it to specific diseases are limited."

The least talked about emotion one can feel during these times of trouble is fear. It is hard to tell someone that you are scared or that you fear. Much like stress, fear can cause some severe damage to the body. I heard this statement from a motivational speech from an unknown author. "Now fear is going to be a player in your life. But you get to decide how much. There's so much power and failure because you learn so much from it."

There is more suffering inside them, like they have failed everyone around them, including themselves. You are a prisoner, and there is no way out. Unless…. you seek out help. It sounds easy enough to reach out. Yet, some do not. I know I did not. I was confused and had nowhere or no one to talk to. One quick push, a moment of bravery, I opened about my feelings. By doing so, it changed my entire world. Letting those emotions build up inside of you will cause more damage and pain. Something unnecessary and be avoided. It is true what people say that there's strength in numbers.

These are the reasons I sought help. I needed a plan on how to accept my situation. I love the phrase, "Live for today, worry about tomorrow, tomorrow." You do not know it but tomorrow could be better than today. Buddha writes, "Each morning, we are born again. What we do today is what matters most." I needed to find myself again, how to be happy. To vanish those who are toxic. To learn how to build boundaries to keep those who make you feel miserable from pouring on the emotional blackmail they use to have the upper hand within the conversation. With those boundaries, I can finally stand up for myself without losing sight of how I want and only accept how someone speaks to me. I deserve respect. I deserve to be happy. And if someone stands in the way of my happiness, then it is time for you to go.

I find that I can no longer play the victim card. The emotions that you hold back from derogatory comments made, whatever they may be. Use those comments of hate and apply them to something you love doing. Be strong. As I reflect on my current life, it is time for me to be strong for the sake of my family. And for me. Authoring this book has made me stronger. A release from feelings I have kept deep down inside of me.

There may be things you currently do that bring you happiness, individual support. You are finding your inner strength and finding joy in the little things in life. Be passionate about your hobbies or ways you find to help you get through your days. Music and sports/ exercising are two of the biggest reasons I will be devoting separate chapters to them. I love to read non-fiction books, especially history and autobiographies. I can no longer read fictional books as I forget the characters and plots. I simply cannot relate to it, nor understand

and remember. I also like to read about certain subjects from all different kinds of views. But I need the actual, physical book, not the ones you buy online. Sorry but I am not going to spend money on an e-book when I can get the real deal for free!!! Remember the line, "Learn all you can?" Knowledge is power.

Help can come in various forms. Support groups either online or in person, consulting with a psychologist or psychiatrist, research, and stay informed with any recent activities. Seeking help through music, sports, exercising (including yoga and meditation), reading, television, I could go on and on. How about your religion? Maybe talking to your Pastor/Father or whoever your beliefs stand for. If what you do is legal and holds some morality, then you are fine. There are a lot of support groups on the Internet. There are support groups for anyone who suffers from an invisible chronic illness, plenty of support groups out there, especially on Facebook. You have exclusive APS & Lupus support groups. But do so carefully. Choosing the right support groups is essential, so look for closed groups, those who invite you to join them. Some will ask simple questions such as your chronic illness. Others may want more information, such as medication(s) you take, etc. If you decide on this route, make sure that they are legitimate and offer a closed group.

As I finish this chapter, I want to list some of my coping mechanisms that help me get through most days. I have two vital areas outside my family life that gives me peace of mind. It gives you extra encouragement to get out of bed and get the day moving. I hope that you, the reader, will enjoy the next two Chapters. I tried bringing out more humor than I had in earlier Chapters. I wanted to keep those on a serious note as they are serious issues to deal with. Not so much with the next two. What does make you happy in life? What kind of things interest you? What you are passionate about in life? Your family? The next two chapters cover two of my passions in life, working out and music.

TEN

My Coping Mechanism #1-Music

"I've done my share of working' out, I want to go
someplace where I can scream and shout,
Show me the lights, where I can find, The only
thing I need to give me peace of mind,
I want to go, I wanna go, I want to go hot rockin'"
Lyrics from the song "Hot Rockin'" by Judas Priest
From the album "Point of Entry" 1981

Please note - This chapter is unaffiliated with both APS and Lupus. I dedicated this chapter to my unique coping mechanisms I use to get through the days. Finally, the opinions expressed are my own for entertainment only.

If you could not tell, I am a music lover. Music for me is exceptionally therapeutic. Certain songs tap into my current emotions, giving me a chance to forget about life for a while. Songs that I sing along to (I am an awful singer). Music with substance. Great vocals, guitars, drums, harmony, singing, and lyrics. Typically, I find the substance in music that is heavier. The type of music I rarely hear on radio. Certain bands and songs that helped me through when life was confusing. At a time, I did not know what I wanted in life. One song in particular, Life of Agony's "Lost at 22", came out when I was 23 years old. The lyrics were a powerful reminder of how life can be when you are young and trying to find your way in life.

> "Well, I'm lost at 22 and I've got no f'ing clue.
> No I don't know if things will work out right.
> I'm lost and confused, I'm lost at 22
> And I don't know if my life's gonna end up right.
> 'Cause they keep on telling me, that I'm young, dumb and naive.
> But that's just what they want me to believe."

I believe that most people would relate to the lyrics when they were twenty-two. This song is an example of how the lyrics of a song need to be powerful. A requirement that still holds true today.

I am a huge fan of Anthrax. Music fans could relate to their songs and lyrics. "Indians" for Indigenous/Native Americans and "Who Cares Win" about the homeless are two outstanding examples. They are known for their energy, musically and on stage. I can attest to their live energy, as I could see them twice in concert. Wow. Incredible shows. But I should have seen them in concert three times.

Anthrax was the opening band for KISS on their "Crazy Nights" tour stop in Madison. Anthrax was on their "Among the Living" tour, one of my favorite Anthrax albums. My friends and I were fifteen and had no drivers' license. A friend of mine's mom was going to take us until she found out the next day was a school day. However, I knew a handful from school who went. On the day of the concert, most were wearing KISS shirts. By the next morning, some were wearing Anthrax shirts. As one put it, "Anthrax blew KISS away." Great.

As a Gen-Xer (Generation X), I grew up when cable television was available with all kinds of channels. One was MTV. Back in its earliest form when they played videos most of the time. All the one-hit wonders with horrific videos. Except for a few bands. Aha's "Take on Me" was a cool video, well ahead of its time. Then some bands had a bunch of videos from a band you never heard of before, like Duran Duran, INXS, John Cougar Mellencamp, The Police. Again, I could go on forever. It was a fun time, music-wise. Case in point, who did not want Mike Score's hairdo from A Flock of Seagulls? The 80s, "The Hairspray Decade." Songs from that era may have been cheesy, but I never tire of listening to that era of music. I have a bunch of MTVs 80s bands/songs on my iPhone. At least one hundred. I know I could produce 75-100 more. I have at least twenty full CDs of eighty's tunes.

The TV channel TBS had the show "Night Tracks," which aired music videos once a week. Each show was three hours long, using airing late at night. I do not recall the type of music videos they aired. But it was "Night Tracks" when I saw a KISS video for the first time. I knew of them through photos, but not their music. The video "Love It Loud," off the album "Creatures of The Night" was played. All I could think of was, "Sweet Mother of God, what am I watching?" What an introduction to KISS.

Trying to listen to anything but pop-rock and country music on the radio was difficult. You could only find a couple of rock stations where I grew up. Local radio stations never played the heavier tunes. Rock stations played classic rock, mostly pre-80s music. Bands like Led Zeppelin, Lynyrd Skynyrd, Deep Purple, and Pink Floyd for examples. One station, 105.7 FM WAPL out of Appleton, WI, slotted heavier music during the "Metal Shop" program with Charlie "The Butcher" Kendall. If I remember right, it ran every Friday night between, "I believe" 10 pm -Midnight on (I am positive on the two-hours). Metal Shop played a great mix of old and new heavier rock/metal.

Often, I would page through either the magazines "Circus" or "Hit Parader" to see any bands that looked out of the ordinary. But they were the only two available. I heard of Kerrang! The problem with Kerrang! was the magazine was from the UK and could not be found. RIP Magazine started in 1988 but was challenging to find. Metal Maniacs, a music magazine that started in 1989, was available to get my hands on. I loved this magazine. They covered more of the thrash bands that were relativity unknown. Perfect. New music worth checking into. But how could you check some of the bands out when they were not played on the radio? Or see their videos? Did the band have videos?

I would like to think that my generation was the earliest form of music sharing, pre-Napster. If you had a dual cassette boom box, you could record music from any band's cassette tape. All you need was a blank (recordable) cassette tape and time. The system could not be any simpler. It was the easiest and cheapest way to do things. You borrowed a tape from someone, and you recorded the songs you liked. All I can say is thank you to those responsible for making the dual cassette boom box to record music.

Like baseball cards, we would tape trade with others. Trading tapes was how I learn about Megadeth. "I believe" I traded ZZ Top's "Eliminator" for Megadeth's "Peace Sells." Whoa. That was a change of pace. To be honest, I was not ready for music that fast. And the guitar riffs were out of this world. How can they play fast and still sound incredible? Within time I was immersed, listening to this tape, following along with the lyrics. At this point, I never knew the bands Anthrax, Metallica, or Slayer existed. It would take my Sophomore Year in High School before I was exposed to them and other bands alike. It took tape trading. Once I listened to them, I fell in love with the music.

Sometimes you had to take a chance. Go to a store, look at the bands album artwork and logo look like and finally the name of the songs. I used this system to find bands that may be worth checking into. The first one that comes to mind is Grim Reaper's "See You in Hell." Whoa. The artwork was incredible. The music, nothing incredible.

I was lucky with my system. But I got burned numerous of times. Tapes I did not like and could not wait to sell. Or it sat collecting dust before I gave it a chance to grow on me. The Summer of 1989 brought my cover artwork system to a screeching halt. I bought Death's "Leprosy" and King Diamond's "Them." I could not believe what I was listening to. One singer growled (Chuck from Death -R.I.P.), and another singer (King Diamond) singing

"Grandma" to the top of his lungs. I was not ready for those types of music. Years went by before I listened to Death's album again and found three songs I liked (Leprosy, Open Casket, and Pull the Plug).

There were other options to learn about heavier bands that you never knew existed. Remember Columbia House Records?? Or BMG? "I believe" you could buy seven, may be more, cassettes for one cent and one at the regular price? It was a cool way to check out bands. You could not beat it. Until you had to buy one at regular price.

MTV's Headbangers Ball was another way to find out different types of bands and their videos. The Headbangers Ball played videos from bands who centered in on specific topics, good or bad, like earthly annihilation (Nuclear Assault's "Critical Mass") to political/government issues (Sacred Reich's "The American Way") to terrible books/movies (Metallica's "One") to statutory rape (Winger's "Seventeen"). Out of two hours, I may see one to three songs/videos worthwhile. That is why I would record (My VCR) the show and skip to videos I wanted to see. One could only manage listing to Skid Row's "I'll Remember You" to Great White's "Once Bitten, Twice Shy" to Poison's "Every Rose Has Its Thorn" to Guns 'N Roses' "Patience" week after week without losing your mind. Terrible.

One of my favorite way to find out about bands and their music style was seeing them in concert, the openers. Bands I have never heard of or took a chance on buying their music. Seeing them in concert brought a whole different perspective when judging their music and how they performed on stage. Most of the openers were great in concert. Good music with a decent stage show. The only drawback was some of the bands I have seen had albums that did not reflect the same energy or attitude. But you had to expect that. Bands will turn it up a notch, playing live in concert.

In 1991, music was changing, and with it, the Headbangers Ball was starting to play a different type of music, which was not what I was used to. The music sounded gritty, plain vocal levels & lyrics that did not make sense. At first, the music was good. The change in music started with, "I believe" the video "We die young" by Alice

In Chains. Great song. Heavy sounding and a great tempo to it. The song received little airplay. Leaving them relatively unknown. Inexplicably, the video for "We Die Young" disappeared and was quickly replaced by their video "Man in the box." A song vastly different in styles, a shift in tempos. In a few months, Alice In Chains, was like a household name. The "Man in the box" video was played throughout the day on MTV, including the Headbangers Ball. Rock stations started playing "Man in the box." Little did I know a shift in the music scene was brewing.

Like Alice In Chains, the same thing happened with the band, Stone Temple Pilots. They had a video for "Sex Type Thing" that was fantastic. Yet little to no airplay. And like Alice In Chains, the video for "Sex Type Thing" disappears, and the video for the song "Plush" appears. A slow, melodic feel to the song. If "Sex type thing" was on one end of the spectrum, "Plush" was the other end. Reminded me of the late 80s. How a band could have a hit single, followed with a power ballad. And due to the redundancy in this system, the band would have their fifteen minutes of fame. And quickly disappeared.

But there was a band to come along and finally killed metal as we know it. A band named Nirvana hit the scene with a video for "Smells like teen spirit." Great song & video. What was weird and hard to understand was those three songs, "Man in the box," "Plush," & "Smells like teen spirit," was not just played on the Headbangers Ball but also in the daily rotation on MTV. Unheard of for metal bands for this to happen. My reasoning why metal died. It was not long before the Headbangers Ball changed their format, and the music term Grunge became the norm.

I was never a grunge fan as it was foreign to me as I could not relate to it. It seemed like every band that was coming out had the same musical riffs, simplistic and repetitive/strange lyrics. No elaborate stage shows. Lacking a certain "look" to them. A come as you are musical approach. Dark and depressing music. Not the music I wanted to listen to. Yet, those bands were changing the music industry.

I am sure that most, if not all, metal bands tried to change with the current times. If they wanted to survive, they needed to change the way they did things or become extinct. The results were not pretty. Band members cut their hair short. Plain looking. No elaborate stage shows. Their videos were not being played because of MTV's Headbangers Ball format change and its slow, painful death. It would take YouTube before I knew bands had videos for their songs during this time.

No band seemed untouchable from changes including Anthrax. They changed singers. The music, lyrics and the production changed. Both albums "Sound of White Noise" and the follow-up album "Stomp 442" were hard to get into. And the album covers were boring. The albums contained a couple of excellent songs, and the rest seemed to me as fillers. It did not help that their record company did a poor job of promoting them. Around this time, I started searching for bands who had their own unique style to them. And hopefully meaningful lyrics. No straightforward task.

I decided maybe it is time to go back to my old method on how to locate bands. Checking out the band's album cover and take a chance if the band was any good. I found one that I loved. The band was New York's Life of Agony and their debut album "River Runs Red." The cool cover hooked me. Somewhere along the way, possibly on MTV's Headbangers Ball, I remembered the song "Through and Through." Wow. I loved the song. Great lyrics, powerful music, and tempo changes. They had their own style called Metal Groove. "Underground" and the album's title "River Runs Red" were great songs as well, containing the same uniqueness. The band's second album, "Ugly," was a step better. Songs like "Lost at 22", "I Regret," & "Damned if I do" are fantastic songs that I could relate to the lyrics. They were the exception to the rule, as I could not find bands worth listening to. Instead of looking forward to new music, why not look backwards to classic bands and their music. Bands like Queen, KISS and most importantly, old school AC/DC.

As a Gen-Xer, there was Queen songs with which I was familiar. Songs "Another one bites the dust" and "We will rock you/We are the champions" were played on radio. Same with "Killer Queen," "Tie your mother down," & "Somebody to love." "Bohemian Rhapsody" was a staple on the radio long before the movie and soundtrack for "Wayne's World" was released. I am sure the movie helped with Queen's record sales.

I purchased both "Classic Queen" and "Greatest Hits" after Freddie Mercury died. Numerous songs on both albums contained songs I loved but forgotten about as radio stations never played them. MTV ignored their videos. Songs like "One Vision" was an excellent song for the movie "Iron Eagle." "I want to break free," with the band in drag (Freddie Mercury vacuum cleaning was funny) and "Who wants to live forever" theme song for "The Highlander" movie. All three ignored but not forgotten in concert.

The Summer of 1992, The Freddy Mercury Concert for Life took place at Wembley Stadium in London, England. A fund raiser and an awareness concert for the AIDS epidemic. The concert was superb. "I believe" my main reason for watching the show on MTV was to see Metallica. But I remember being impressed by Extreme and their mix of different Queen songs. The night's best performance was The Who's Roger Daltrey, with Queen doing "I want it all." Awesome. They could not have picked a better frontman to sing the song.

What seemed to be instantaneously, I rented the VHS tape "Queen – Live at Wembley." Wow, what a performance. They opened the show with "One Vision." And played the before mentioned songs "I want to break free" and "Who wants to live forever." Freddie had the crowd in the palm of his hand. Singing along with him, word for word. Search the song "Love of my life" on YouTube. What a voice. Freddie Mercury was definitely one of the best frontmen in Rock 'N Roll history.

KISS would be another band that gave me a chance to explore their older 70s songs/albums. I certainly knew KISS, starting with the "Creatures of the Night" album. "War Machine" was an excellent song that a lot of people do not know existed. Then the makeup came off. Songs like "Lick It Up," "Heavens on Fire," & "Tears are

Falling" could be heard everywhere, including on MTV. The older songs were nowhere to be found.

I still remember buying "Smashes, Thrashes, and Hits" tape. I recognized some of their older songs, like "Love Gun," "Deuce," and "Detroit Rock City." Over time, exposure to more of their older music, songs like "Firehouse," "God of Thunder," and "I stole your love," for starters. I finally heard the original "Parasite," a song Anthrax covered on their "Attack of the Killer B's" album. In 1994, I bought both CD & VHS tape "KISS MY ASS." A comprehensive arrangement of bands covering KISS songs. Anthrax appears on both doing "She," produced by no other than Gene & Paul of KISS. I was lucky enough to see KISS on their Reunion Tour, August of 1996. $57 per ticket, if I remember correctly. What a show. If they could have swapped out a couple of songs, like "Kings of the Nighttime World" and "Watchin' You" for "I Stole Your Love." If they could have had Anthrax opening the show.

I have always been an AC/DC fan since I was ten or eleven. Every Summer, my hometown baseball teams would have two games (Little League 8-12 years old) per week, one home game and one away. When we had away games, most of the time, it seemed AC/DC's "Dirty Deeds Done Dirt Cheap" tape would be blaring from someone's boom box on the school bus. Since it was Summer, all the windows on the bus were down. When it came time for the song "Big Balls," we would be yelling "But we got the biggest balls of them all" out of the windows. It still makes me laugh to this day.

Beyond their "Dirty Deeds" album, I had little to no exposure to the Bon Scott era. Radio stations would only play the song "Highway to Hell," and that was it. But the "Back in Black" album, you could hear half of the album on radio and catch live versions of "Back in Black" & "Hell's Bells" videos on MTV's mainstream play. At this point in my life, I assumed AC/DC had one singer, Brian Johnson. A tall, tough guy, menacing look with a bandana tied around his neck, wearing a Harley Davidson t-shirt and a newsboy cap/hat.

Out of nowhere, the video for "Jailbreak" was released, and was played on MTV. It was weird. The band was playing on a rock pile—two guys dressed as corrections officers playing guitars. Angus Young is playing his guitar while wearing the ugliest pajamas humanly possible. Bon swinging a sledgehammer. Plus, the song seemed different from the songs I have seen and heard before. But where did this singer come from? It was a head scratcher. Did they change singers?

Eventually, I found out that AC/DC had another singer that died before "Back in Black" was released. The singer (Bon Scott) sang on both "Dirty Deeds" and on "Highway to Hell." I never put two and two together. Another album I never get tired of listening to "Highway to Hell." There were great songs that I never heard. In my humble opinion, "Highway to Hell" album is a masterpiece. Songs "Girls got Rhythm," "Walk all over you," "Touch too much," and one of my favorites, "If you want Blood (You got it), easily support my admission.

Little at a time, my Bon Scott era of AC/DC CD collection would start to grow. I bought the album "High Voltage," "Powerage," and "Let There Be Rock." Once they released the five CD box set, appropriately named "Bonfire," it did not take long before I bought it. What a collection of rare gems. An expanded "Let There Be Rock." Live recordings at the Atlantic Records studio. Different versions of songs, including different lyrics and song title. Indeed, a must-have for old-school, Bon Scott era AC/DC fans.

There happens to be some who believe that Bon Scott wrote the lyrics on the "Back in Black" album. I am a believer. Listen closely to the lyrics. Those lyrics closely resemble Bon's writing style on "Highway to Hell." Compare the song titles. Who could you envision coming up with them? Bon used lyrics which involve knifes, guns, explosions, fast cars (usually Cadillacs), unique references about his privates and of course, drinking. Can you picture Bon writing the song, "Have a drink on me?" Not convinced, read the eye-opening book, "Bon: The Last Highway; The Untold Story of Bon Scott and AC/DC's Back in Black" by Jessie Fink. A great book, must-read for all AC/DC fans. After "Black in Black," I thought their albums started to nosedive in creativity. In my opinion, losing Bon Scott was the reason.

I like to finish this chapter in my unique way. No better way to end this chapter with fun facts concerning various thoughts involved with the music I love or hate. Again, this is merely my opinion. Here we go:

1. I like three Depeche Mode songs: "Enjoy the Silence" (My favorite), "People are People," & "Personal Jesus." Really. Not exactly my favorite type in music.

2. Ed Sheeran's song "Perfect" is perfect. I love the lyrics, the harmony, the passion in his voice, the light music in the background. Reminds me how Phil Collins sang "Against All Odds" with unbelievable passion.

3. Best concert = Suicidal Tendencies, Exodus, and Pantera, in August 1990.

4. I hate attending concerts with extended guitar/drum solos. If I am at a show, I came to listen to the band play their songs, so I get my money's worth. Not listen to 15-20 minutes of solos (drums, guitar, and some band's bass guitar) as I already know you can play. I can manage solos for a couple of minutes, as I figure this is a way for the band to change out guitars, get something to drink, etc. Which I can understand. But enough with the long, drawn-out solos already.

5. I do not care if this song is cheesy, but I like Judas Priest's "Turbo Lover." Just the song and not the video.

6. Why did Atlantic Records omit the song "Torture Tactics" by Vio-Lence off their "Oppressing the Masses" album? I know it originally included the song upon the album's release but was soon recalled/destroyed. The lyrics are brutal and could be offensive to others, describing the punishment ensued with torture. Who cares? It is a great song. Think about the potential fans who could have purchased the album if they included it on the album. "Torture Tactics" was released as an EP. What a waste. Big mistake by Atlantic Records.

7. I like Metallica, but I will not listen to the Black Album to their present-day music. Give me "Master of Puppets" any day of the week.

8. Of all the cassettes/CD's I have ever owned throughout the past thirty plus years, here is a list of some of the worst or confusing album covers I have issues with:

   • Metallica's "Black Album." From cool covers on back-to-back albums "Master of Puppets" to "And...Justice for All," we are given an album cover like AC/DC's "Back in Black" or the "Spinal Tap Official Movie Soundtrack." It is also a shame they did not have Bob Rock around to produce "And...Justice for All."

   • As much of an Anthrax fan I am, I must call out the album cover of "Stomp 442". No Anthrax logo, a man is standing with his bare ass and a massive ball of crushed vehicles. The production stinks. The song "Fueled" is the only song pushed by the record company/management (I think). In my opinion, "Random Acts of Senseless Violence" and "American Pompeii" are better.

   • WASP's "The Last Command" album cover is beyond words to describe other than crap. The logo on the "Animal" is incredible. The cast iron/metal looking logo with screws placed all around the logo is fantastic. The logo on their debut album is cool. But what happened on "The Last Command"? Is this the best they could do. W.A.S.P. spelled out on an Orange/Tan background with only Blackie Lawless (Vocalist) on the cover, far away from the camera. The lettering looks like it came from a children's book. The cover from "Inside the Electric Circus" is not much better. Another album cover is featuring only Blackie Lawless. So much for the other three guys. At least the logo looks better than the one on "The Last Command."

   • Flotsam and Jetsam have a great logo featured on both "Doomsday for the Deceiver" and "No Place for

Disgrace." What happened to the logo on the album "When the Storm comes down" album? Awful.

- The original cover of KISS' "Creatures of the Night." Why did they change it on the reissue? I heard Paul Stanley say something along the line as "Why feature someone (Ace Frehley) on the cover who never played on the album"? The reissue has Bruce Kulick on the cover, and he did not play on the album.

- Exodus's original cover for "Pleasures of the Flesh." Why change it? Did the record company or management had something to do with it? Huge mistake by the record company. Think about the amount of merchandise sold, the money made over the years. I love the bar name, "Cannibal Bar & Grill."

- As I finish, let me ask you this critical question. Have you ever seen a lousy album cover from Iron Maiden? Trick question as it has never happened. They are all cool— Unique from their prior albums. Remember the cool t-shirts from the songs "The Trooper" & "Aces High"? I would have killed for those. "Long live Eddie!"

ELEVEN

My Coping Mechanisms #2- Exercising

"Going to the gym and training was a tremendous resource
of therapy for me. It was probably the single most important
therapeutic choice I could make on my own, in my own personal
life. Recognizing that if I did not do that, it was not anyone's fault
but my own. My bodybuilding experience taught me that I could
be successful, I can be a failure, but I'm in the driving seat."
Kai Greene – "Generation Iron (Movie)"

Please note - This Chapter is unaffiliated with both APS and
Lupus. I dedicated this Chapter to my unique coping mechanisms
I use to get through the days. Finally, the opinions expressed are my
own for entertainment only.

One of the first sports movie that caught my attention as a kid
was Rocky 2. I never watched the first one before viewing Rocky
2. I am guessing sometime back in the late '70s or possibly the early
'80s. VHS or Beta tapes did not exist. I watched this movie at our
city's library, which had a laserdisc player. Remember those? The
discs were the size of vinyl records. They were huge. They served
their purpose, and that is all that matters.

I was in awe over how Rocky trained. It was fascinating how he
introduced himself. The determination to win after Adrianne gave
him permission after coming out of her coma. The one-arm pushups,

Rocky was going to town on the jump rope and tossing it aside when finishing. The look of determination after. The eye of the tiger. It was a huge motivator and left a permanent impression on me. The movie clips and the music got my blood thumping.

As a few years went by and watching other Sylvester Stallone movies, such as Rocky 3, First Blood, and Rambo: First Blood Part Two, Sylvester was God. To look like he did in those movies was merely inconceivable. Really. Skinny and muscular. It was pure insanity. You ask a hundred guys who grew up during that era and ask them if they would have wanted to look like him. I bet half would say yes. Those memories of Stallone etched a memory and a motivational factor that would stay with me for the rest of my life.

Unless you have lived under a rock, you know the name Hulk Hogan from the pro wrestling genre. He was huge—Mr. All American within the WWF (World Wrestling Federation). But muscle-wise, it was The Ultimate Warrior who caught my eye. Talk about built like a brick. Now that is what I wanted to be. Either him or Stallone. Or a little of both.

Lastly, there was another WWF Tag Team that motivated me to lift. The Road Warriors/Legion of Doom were monsters. Holy crap. First, you had Animal, real name was Joseph Laurinaitis (R.I.P. Sept. 2020). He was the powerlifter, former bouncer. One look at Animal, you understood his power—a solid mass of humanity. Secondly, you had Michael Hegstrand (R.I.P. Oct. 2003) as Hawk. He had a muscular look. Hawk had traps (Trapezius – Muscles in your upper back, neck area) to kill for. They were awesome.

I beg you to bring up their pre-match Introduction, coming down to ringside on YouTube. You had Hawk's introduction "Blah…. What a Rush"! Then the music kicks in. Watching them coming down to ringside, wearing makeup and football shoulder pads with spikes. No smiling. Pure determination to destroy anyone in their way (match). Their determination, to me, was serious motivation.

Like kids in a small town, we all played sports. But how did you keep in shape. Thankfully, we did not have Xbox's or Playstation's to control our every waking moment. All you could do to keep in shape were the basics, running, pull-ups, and pushups. We had no weights sets or machines to use. That would change for our household when my parents bought a DP Workout Bench including 100 to 110 totals in weights.

Working out with our DP weights was clumsy and bothersome. It was hard to change the thick weights, two inches in width on a narrow-sized barbell. They were huge. If I remember right, you could not place all of them on the rack. The bench was too narrow to do proper bench presses. At my age, I did not know any better. You followed the guidelines listed on their poster-sized paper.

After a while, "I believe" in 1991, I bought 100 lbs. worth of narrow plates and another set of locks for the DP barbell. This way, I could move the starting point where I wanted the weights. Place one set of locks at arm's width, then the plates, and lastly, the other set of locks. Now I was safely able to set up the bar to perform presses. Add different exercises (barbell curls), and I was ready for the year. My body was changing, and with it, my strength. If I wanted to keep pushing myself to get bigger and stronger, I needed to make a change.

I started a membership with the National Fitness and Wellness Center in Beaver Dam, WI., lasting five years. The gym had everything I needed to move forward with my training and help me reach my goals. Around the same time, I fell in love with bodybuilding. My desire to learn led to buying magazine subscriptions to Muscle & Fitness and the WBF's (World Bodybuilding Federation) publication. I liked the WBF, including their Saturday morning TV show on the USA Channel. Due to a steroid scandal that rocked the WWF, and the lack of interest from the bodybuilding industry, the WBF disbanded.

I may have like WBF's magazine, but Muscle & Fitness was better. Muscle & Fitness covered the entire industry. Featuring article upon article of valuable training tips. One of the more significant features at the time was the current Mr. Olympia, Lee Haney. Lee looked incredible. Perfect symmetry. I also took to heart what he said back then, "Isolate the muscle, not annihilate." Very profound statement coming from the eight-time Mr. Olympia champion.

Another profound statement that I love is Kai Greene's quote, "I can be successful, I can be a failure, but I am in the driving seat." There is no one to blame for coming up short on goals. I based my monthly goals on how much I was lifting (no matter the exercise). To conduct my monitoring, I would write everything down within a notebook. I did not want to rely on memory to know what I accomplished or what I failed to improve upon. Through my notebook, I would study my notes and see if a particular exercise were beneficial. Maybe I needed to tweak a few things, such as using a different grip, change the angle of my moment or go from free weights to machines. Keeping an open mind then has had a considerable impact on how I exercise today.

Working out at a gym is no longer feasible, living in a small city. I have used a Bowflex, resistant rod training for over twenty years. The Bowflex is easier on my muscles and joints. Plus, the Bowflex is readily available. No longer waiting for weights or machines to open.

As I lift today, not much has changed with my lifting style, other than the rep changes and avoiding maxing out. I keep the reps over fifteen while using a weight that I can control throughout the process, including breathing. I learned a tremendous number of skills throughout the years, what works, what does not, how you should be lifting instead of subjecting your body to injury. One of my most significant rules was form. There is no substitute for form. My belief was and has always been to control the weight, do not let the weight control you. "Isolate not annihilate." Simply put, no cheating!!! An example would be barbell curls, which is an isolation movement. The main muscles used are your biceps and forearms. I never believed that you should be swaying your body to lift heavier. To me, your elbows need to stay back, just at the sides of your hips and curl. Only your arms should be doing the work. Over twenty years, this became my MO. (modus operandi) and my body adapted to those methods.

As I write this, it is weird to think that I have been working out, lifting weights, anaerobic exercising for nearly two-thirds of my life. My working out ways have drastically changed throughout the years. My health has become a significant source of caution while exercising. I find working out therapeutic. It gives you something to look forward to, a purpose, a goal. You can forget about life for a while. A great way to take out your frustrations. Ex-UFC champion Connor McGregor describes his training as a "sick sense of security." I feel the same way.

Once I fully understood my heart condition, I made drastic changes to my resistance training routine. I have been using a Bowflex Extreme for ten years and have made some additions to help maximize my sets, such as adding an extra 100lbs. of resistance. I kept my reps between 6-10, with the last set to failure, the method of maxing out. But those were the days before my heart condition. Things needed to change, including my stubbornness for lifting heavy, the "Go heavy or go home" motto.

I had a sit down with my Cardiologist to discuss some of the challenges I face, and the changes needed, for starters, changing my rep range to 15 to 20. She asked me point blank if I have already achieved all my goals. I only had one, bench pressing 315 lbs., which I was successful doing. Her reply was, "What more do you have to prove"? I could not answer her. I never had any further bench-pressing goals as 315 lbs. was enough. I always had excellent leg strength, thunder thighs. But I do not recall ever having or setting a goal. Deep down, I am sure I did not. I was never fond of squats as I wanted to preserve my knees as best as humanly possible. Playing catcher in baseball for seven to eight years took its' toll on my knees.

I have always felt from the first time I started lifting that flexibility was king. I would be stretching during sets. Most athletes need strength, power, explosive speed to be competitive. You can have all the strength in the world, but you still need flexibility. Anything that you can do to keep your body from tightening up or unneeded joint pain/pressure. Flexibility is a must.

I like to walk on my treadmill when my body allows me to. I make sure that I have my knee brace on, shoes that never get worn other than for the treadmill, and my heart monitor when I remember to place it on. No running as my body cannot manage it. But I have always hated running, especially on a treadmill. Rough on my knees.

We have our treadmill in the basement. We placed it in an area in the middle to the television and our old entertainment receiver with five surround sound speakers hanging from the ceiling right above the treadmill. Along with a DVD player and an Amazon Firestick. You can quickly lose yourself while watching TV while walking. Time can fly by. Before you know it, you just walked for 30 minutes & nearly completed one or two shows at the same time. Great way to get caught up on some of your favorite shows that your spouse does not watch or like.

One of my biggest hurdles has been feeling guilty that I cannot function like you used to. I had those feelings when I was still in the workforce. At times, I would have so much fatigue that there was no way I was getting behind the wheel of a vehicle. Times when I was not mentally sharp. Simply put, it just was not there. To make matters worse, you feel guilty. I felt that same way when I would work out—having the belief that I should work out every day. Be able to stick to a schedule. Or stick to a diet. That is my biggest weakness. My kryptonite.

Someone worth checking out is C.T. Fletcher. You can find useful videos on YouTube with C.T. But beware, he drops a lot of F-Bombs. One of my favorite videos is titled "Last Will and Testament." He talks about what motivates him. He specifically points out two athletes. One who was in his late sixties and one who has MS (Multiple Sclerosis). C.T. sites the stories of overcoming the odds, things they should not have survived or live with daily. Yet they keep finding purpose, the motivation that keeps them going.

The company Generation Iron has produced a handful of documentaries, all of them are great. They made a complete documentary about C.T. Fletcher titled "C.T. Fletcher: My Magnificent Obsession." Everything he has done in life, his upbringing, his achievements, and his heart issues. It seems like he has been through enough for one person. Yet he keeps going, pushing himself to be a monster in the gym. His unorthodox training and the body he created. Amazing. I cannot say it enough. Do you need motivation? Watch one of his YouTube videos.

It is hard when you are at home most, if not all day. Then add my health to the factor. To stay in shape is near impossible. I had a Doctor who said that losing weight while on my current medication would be tough to do. The side effects listed on a couple of the pill bottles states, "Weight gain could be a factor" or something along those lines. Over eight years, I have gained 35-40 lbs. If I cannot work out on either the treadmill or my Bowflex, my diet needs to be perfect. Or eat as little as possible—no carbs from sugar. Eat anything that has large amounts of fiber. Slow to digest. Easier said than done.

C.T. Fletcher, from the Bodybuilders.com website, produced his Ten Commandments of lifting. He calls it out. C.T. will say what is on his mind and backs up those words in the gym. If you look at him, you agree that the man knows what he is talking about. To have some fun as I close out this chapter, I thought it would be fun to post my Ten Commandments while having two autoimmune diseases.

MY TEN COMMANDMENTS

1. **Food is fuel.**

   Eating clean and sticking to a diet is essential. The older you get, the tougher it becomes. Your body is one of a kind. It may or may not respond to certain foods that are considered essential. One size does not fit all. Even specific named diets such as the Keto or Vegan diets may not work. I would suggest talking to a dietician. I found out that my protein levels were too high and placing stress on my kidneys. Yikes. Soon after, my lab results, I cut my protein in half.

2. **Listen to your body all day long.**

   Listening to your body is just as important as the First Commandment. Whether you did something wrong, over-doing it, not feeling rested, muscle stiffness can occur throughout the day. You must ask yourself; Did I eat clean (correctly)? Did I follow my workout plan? Did I push myself too hard, more than your last workout? If you happen to start a movement and cannot feel a pump (isolate the muscle), stop. Your body is telling you that it is not there today. Your brain is saying, "Yes, I feel energized and ready to go," but your body is saying, "I can't get my muscles to concentrate on isolating." It would be best to stop before you regret things such as getting injured, for starters. Just chalk it up as you tried, but I could not do it. Remember, there is always tomorrow.

3. **<u>Make every rep count.</u>**

I talked about this subject before about "Isolate, not annihilate." Your reps should not be sloppy or out of control. Control the weight, do not let it control you.

4. **<u>Change routines often.</u>**

I will be honest as I stole this from C.T. As he said, "Our bodies are magnificent creations." If you perform the same exercises time and time again, your body will adapt to it. However, if you change the exercises around, your body will have to learn to adapt. Altering angles can prove to be the most effective. Your body will not have the ability to adapt. That is precisely what you want unless you overdo things.

5. **<u>Experiment (What works for you).</u>**

This Commandment goes hand in hand with the previous one. As a resistant trainer, I will use a resistant band for arm exercises. Reverse forearm curls are my favorite while using the bands. I can isolate the muscles better than I can while using the Bowflex. Overhead crunches are also more comfortable using the bands. Throw them overhead a steel beam, two-by-four, whatever. Just as effective as using the rope on top of the Bowflex.

6. **Stretch, stretch, and stretch some more.**

I cannot emphasize enough when it comes to stretching. Regardless of who you are or what you do during exercising, stretching is essential. In resistant training, performing a couple of sets of warmups will help loosen up the muscles. Intend of using—light weights. For me, working chest and shoulders, I got to stretch. And I do them in-between every set. Having a lousy right rotator cuff will do that. And keeping it loose and relaxed will help me perform the movement that satisfies me. Remember, I am strict when it comes to movements.

7. **Spot Training does not work.**

Think about your body as a vehicle's engine. If you do not properly maintain the engine, it breaks down. You cannot ignore proper maintenance and expect the engine to run at full capacity. In training/working out, you cannot ignore a body part and expect your whole body to respond or look the way you want it to be. The number one body part that I have ignored is abdominal muscles. And still is. I do not know why. It is hard work. And they are boring.

8. **Do not give in to exercise gimmicks, so-called "Fitness Pro's," or exercise equipment.**

Remember the Thigh Master with Suzanne Sommers as its spokesperson? Do you believe that this machine will ail all your workout issues? How about all the DVDs that are on the market? Remember Richard Simmons' "Sweating to the oldies?" Do not get me wrong, some are legit and work the body. But most, if not all, will not instruct you how to eat effectively. Go back and reread Commandment #1.

9. **<u>Find what motivates you.</u>**

Go back and reread the part concerning C.T Fletcher. Ask yourself, what motivates me? Mine is easy, but it is difficult to achieve. Every hour of every day is an adventure. Do I have the energy to work out, even if it is only 15 minutes (1/4 of your workout) long? Woke up exhausted and cannot get rid of it? Do I have a headache, or does one develop when I work out? Are my muscles or joints sore? That is a mental workout. Just do your best. That is all anyone, including yourself, could ask for.

10. **<u>Have fun and enjoy the process.</u>**

If something is not fun to do, then why are you doing it? But is there a way to make it fun? Working out is a lot like that. Thinking about the grind and avoiding the motivation, you started doing this in the first place. Having a great body will not happy overnight. Think baby steps. Remember, the process is not a sprint. It is a marathon. Simply put, enjoy everything life has to offer, including working out.

GOODBYE, FAREWELL,
AND THE END

✂

"From a humble beginning to a humble ending."

After three years, I can honestly say I am done. I had a lot to say. A lot to think about: to accumulate my memories, good and bad. All the struggles. The disappointments. How to write from a man's point of view. To be open, honest, and not afraid to hold anything back. The time invested. All the notes I have written. The constant struggle to reread each Chapter. The "Brain Drain," when there is nothing left to write. Or so you think. I am making corrections and coming full circle to how difficult it is to draft a book.

Trust me, lots of sentences and paragraphs have been dropped along the way. Naturally, the words did not convey a message or thought I was striving for. Placing thoughts into words has never been a strength and will stay the same. I cannot envision drafting more books. Blogs could be a possibility. Team with someone with the same health issues and start a podcast. My podcast. The thought makes me laugh.

Not much left to add to this Chapter, other than thanking and expressing my gratitude to those who have helped make this book a reality. Thank You to my family, especially my wife and my children. I love you all. Thank you to my brother and his wife, my sister and her husband. We have been through a lot over the last couple of years. Thank you to Tina Pohlman for all your help concerning my health and the never-ending guidance. Thank you for Desia Xiong for the awesome APS and Lupus Fighter Logo. Thank you for all the positive voices I have around me. By far, the biggest Thank You goes to my mother and father. I hope I made you proud!

In the fame words of comedian George Burns, "Say Goodnight, Gracie."